Adventures with Small Animals

Owen Bishop

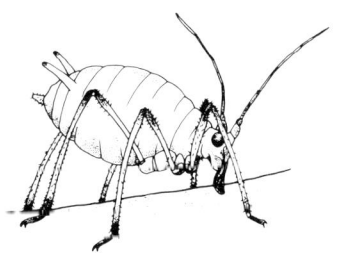

John Murray

Other books in the Adventures series

Digital Electronics
Electronics
Microelectronics
Physics

By the same author

Natural Communities
Outdoor Biology (Teachers' Guide and 3 Pupils' Books)

Acknowledgement

I am grateful to Norman Parker, of the Biology Department of Millfield School, for his skill and enthusiasm in producing the illustrations for this book.

© O. N. Bishop 1982

First published 1982
by John Murray (Publishers) Ltd
50 Albemarle Street, London W1X 4BD

All rights reserved.
Unauthorised duplication
contravenes applicable laws

Made and printed in Great Britain by
Fletcher & Son Ltd, Norwich
Set in Monophoto Plantin

British Library Cataloguing in Publication Data
Bishop, O. N.
  Adventures with small animals.
  1. Animals—Studying and Teaching
  I. Title
  591   QL51.1
  ISBN 0–7195–3944–7   ISBN 0–7195–3930–7 Pbk

Contents

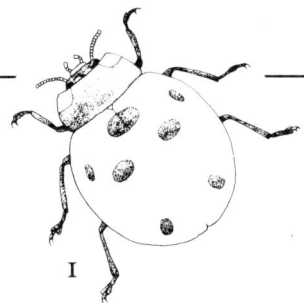

The lives of small Animals — 1

1 Spider's webs — 2
2 A mini-aquarium — 7
3 Collecting galls — 13
4 The life of aphids — 18
5 A water-drop microscope — 22
6 A wormery — 28
7 Keeping caterpillars — 32
8 Life in leaves and soil — 37
9 Making a microhabitat — 42
10 The world of the woodlouse — 45
11 Breeding flour beetles — 50
12 Keeping ants — 55

Results of breeding flour beetles — 58

Some useful books and equipment suppliers — 60

The lives of small animals

It is impossible in a book of this size to describe the vast number of small animals and the lives that they lead. What we can do, however, is to concentrate on the commonest group of small animals (in fact the commonest group of all animals), the insects, and study their life-cycles.

Insects can have one of two main types of life-cycle. Some such as the butterflies, moths, beetles, ants and flies have four stages to their life-cycle. The first stage is the *egg* which hatches to give a *larva*. Larvae of butterflies and moths are called *caterpillars*; larvae of flies are often called *maggots*. The larvae feed and grow, shedding their skins several times. When they are fully grown they become *pupae*. The pupa of a butterfly is called a *chrysalis*. In this stage they neither feed nor move, while inside they are busily re-organizing their bodies. Eventually, the skin of the pupa splits open and the *adult*, or *imago*, emerges. The adult usually has wings and can reproduce. It feeds in order to supply itself with energy, but it does not grow. Male and female adults mate, the females lay eggs, and the cycle begins all over again.

The other main type of life-cycle is followed by insects such as the aphids, grasshoppers, dragon-flies and mayflies. The eggs of these insects hatch to give a *nymph* (sometimes called a larva), which looks similar to the adult, but is smaller, has no wings, cannot reproduce, and is often slightly different in its bodily proportions and has different markings. The nymph feeds and grows, moulting its skin several times. There are several nymph stages. At the last moult, the adult emerges with wings and the ability to reproduce. Male and female adults mate, the females lay eggs, and the cycle begins all over again. Some insects such as the aphids (Chapter 4) leave out the egg stage at certain seasons of the year, the females giving birth to small nymphs.

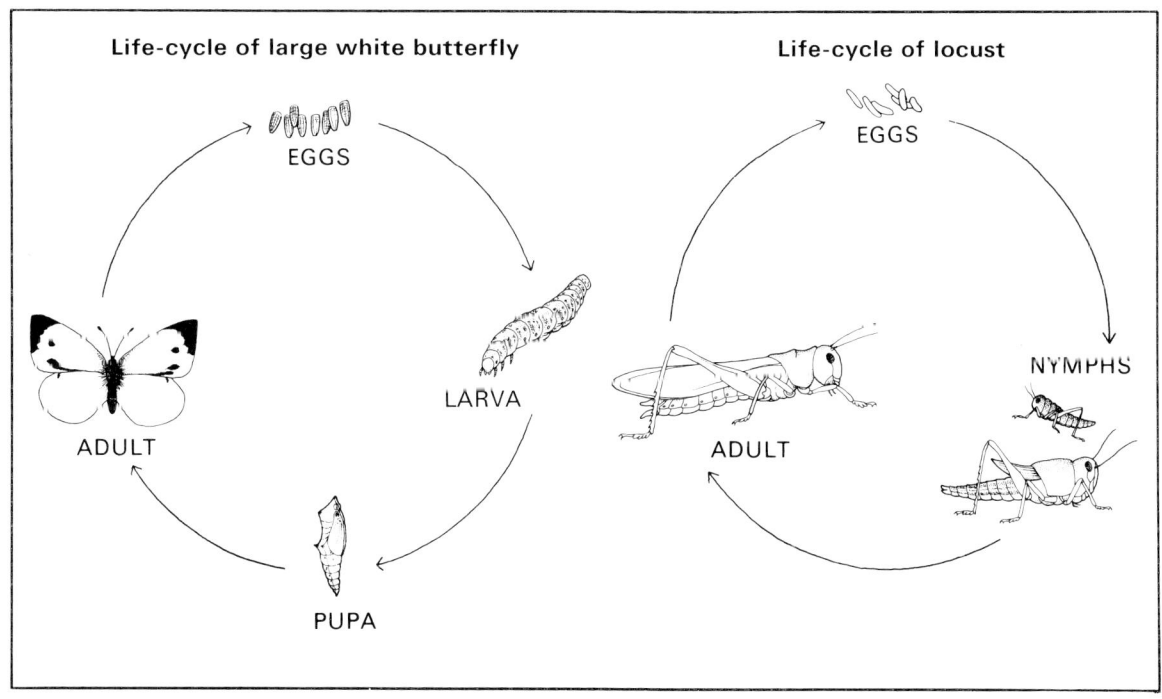

1 Spiders' webs

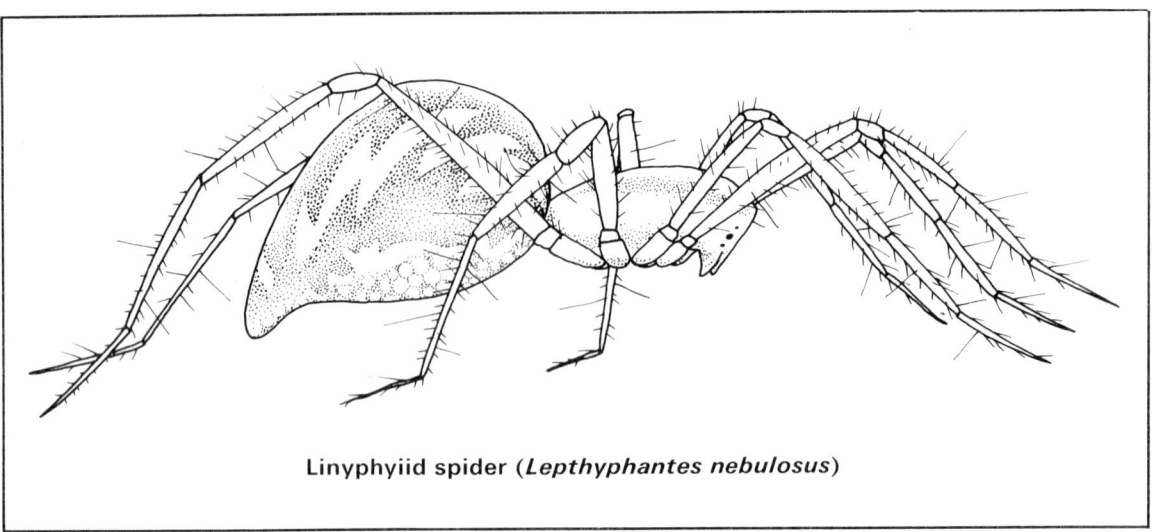

Linyphyiid spider (*Lepthyphantes nebulosus*)

Spiders are carnivores, feeding on other small animals, particularly insects. *Wolf spiders* which live on the ground and can run fast chase their prey. *Jumping spiders*, on the other hand, stalk their prey or perhaps stay hidden and wait for it to pass close by. Then they jump on to their prey, paralyse it and feed on it. Many other spiders catch their prey by building webs, and these are the kinds of spiders you will be studying in this chapter. Spiders may be found at most times of the year except during the coldest weather. The best months are August and September.

WHAT YOU NEED

A large container for housing the spider (see opposite, *Making the cage*); two small containers, one with a lid, such as small jam jars or pickle jars—one is to catch the spiders in, the other is to hold water for the twigs; a shallow container such as the plastic lid of a food pack, to hold the water supply; some fresh leafy twigs; some well-branched leafless twigs; soil; a metre or two of iron wire, about 1 mm diameter; pieces of black cardboard; Copydex or similar adhesive.

MAKING THE CAGE

The main points about the cage are:

1 It must be large enough for the spider to build its web in. If you measure a web built outdoors, you will know how large the cage must be.

2 It must be able to hold a layer of damp soil at the bottom.

3 It should *preferably* have clear glass or plastic on all sides so that you can view the web clearly.

You may be able to find a suitable container ready-made. A glass or plastic aquarium is ideal, or you may have a large jar or plastic sandwich box that can be put to use. Seed trays with tall transparent plastic covers (sold as 'propagators') also make good cages.

Perhaps you would prefer to make your own cage. The drawing shows two simple designs. Be ready to adapt these designs (as well as all other designs in this book) to make use of bits and pieces that you already have handy. Readiness to improvise and make use of scraps saves money that can be

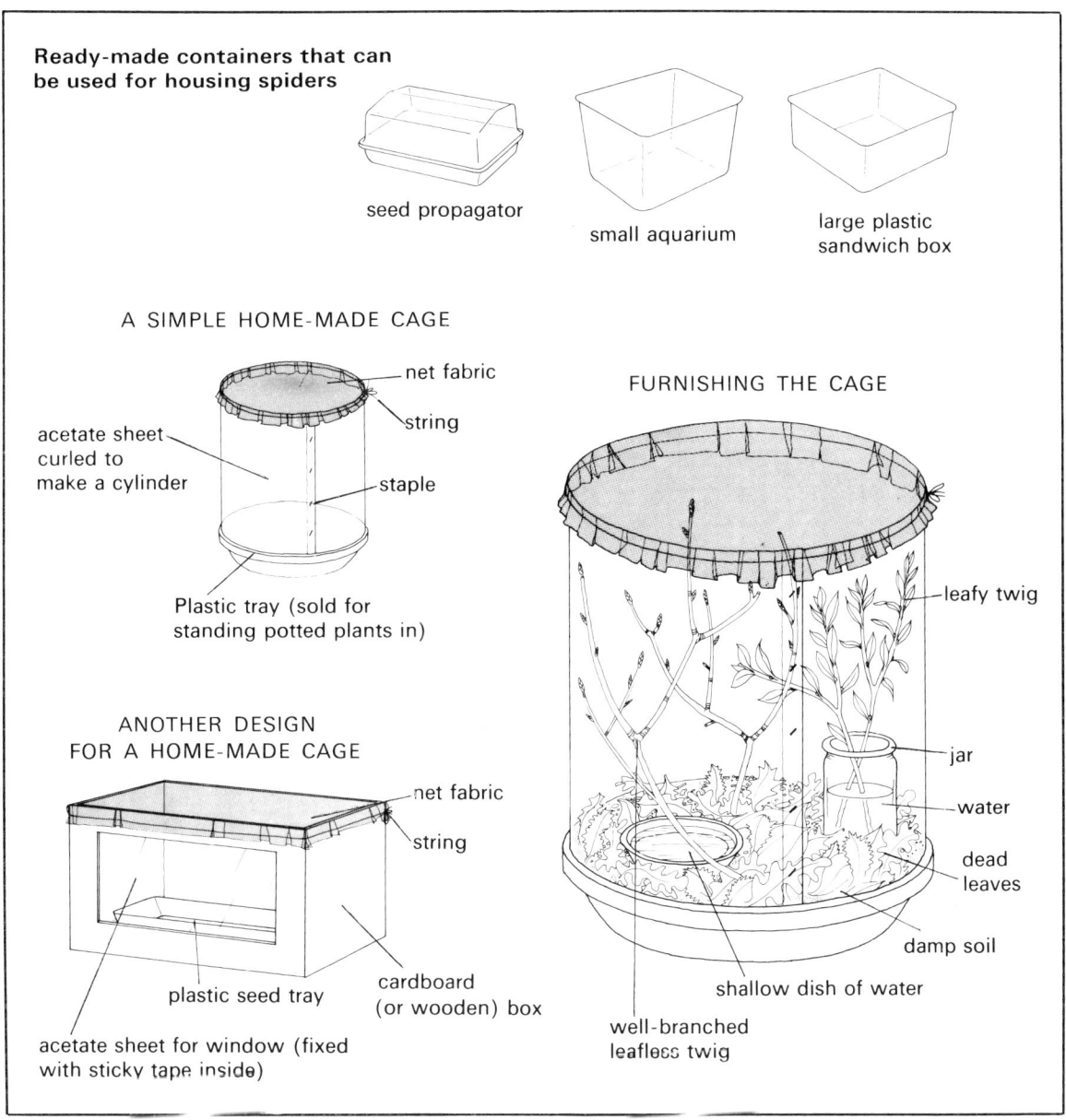

better spent on things you *cannot* make for yourself.

The top of the cage is covered with nylon or terylene netting tied with string—you could use a scrap from an old net curtain.

GETTING STARTED

An important point to remember is that spiders need damp conditions at all times, so put the cage where it will not tend to dry out. Choose a spot where it will not have direct sunlight falling on it and where it will not be overheated by a radiator or other room-heater.

To catch a web-building spider, look for a web in the early morning after a still cool night when there will be dew on the web, which glistens in the early morning sunshine. On a frosty autumn morning webs may readily be seen because of the frost on them. Under other conditions you will need to look a little more carefully.

Since spiders generally live in damp places, good spots to look are: inside sheds and outhouses; on areas of long grass; on the lower or shady sides of hedges; on greenhouses, especially under the staging; among the lower branches of trees; under large stones.

As some spiders only come out when it is dark, take a torch and go searching in the evening.

When you have found the web, the next thing is to find the spider. The spider may be on the web, perhaps waiting in one corner of it for a fly to become caught. If the spider is not to be seen, try tapping the web gently a few times. The spider will sense the vibrations coming along its signal thread and come out of hiding to investigate. Some spiders hide in a handy crevice in the bark of a tree; some hide beneath a leaf; and other spiders build a funnel as part of their web and hide in that.

It is usually easy to catch spiders because when disturbed they often drop quickly off the web. Just hold the open jar beneath the web and the spider will probably drop straight into it.

If you have *two* spiders in a cage, it is likely that one will kill and eat the other. So when you have caught *one* spider, bring it home and put it in the cage. Fill the shallow container with water, so that the air in the cage is kept damp, and tie the netting securely across the top of the cage. Then wait for web-building to begin.

WEB-BUILDING

Watch your spider as it builds its web. The webs of *orb web spiders* are built to a definite pattern that varies in detail from species to species. The main stages are usually as follows:

1 Stretching out the main radial threads, attached to the twig or other supports. How many main radial threads are there?

2 Bridging the outer ends of these spiral threads to form the outline of the web.

3 Putting in more radial threads. How many?

4 Making a small strengthening mat of threads at the centre of the web.

5 Spinning a spiral to strengthen the net. How many turns has the spiral? Does the spider begin in the centre and move outwards down the spiral, or does it begin at the outside and work inwards? Does it go clockwise or anti-

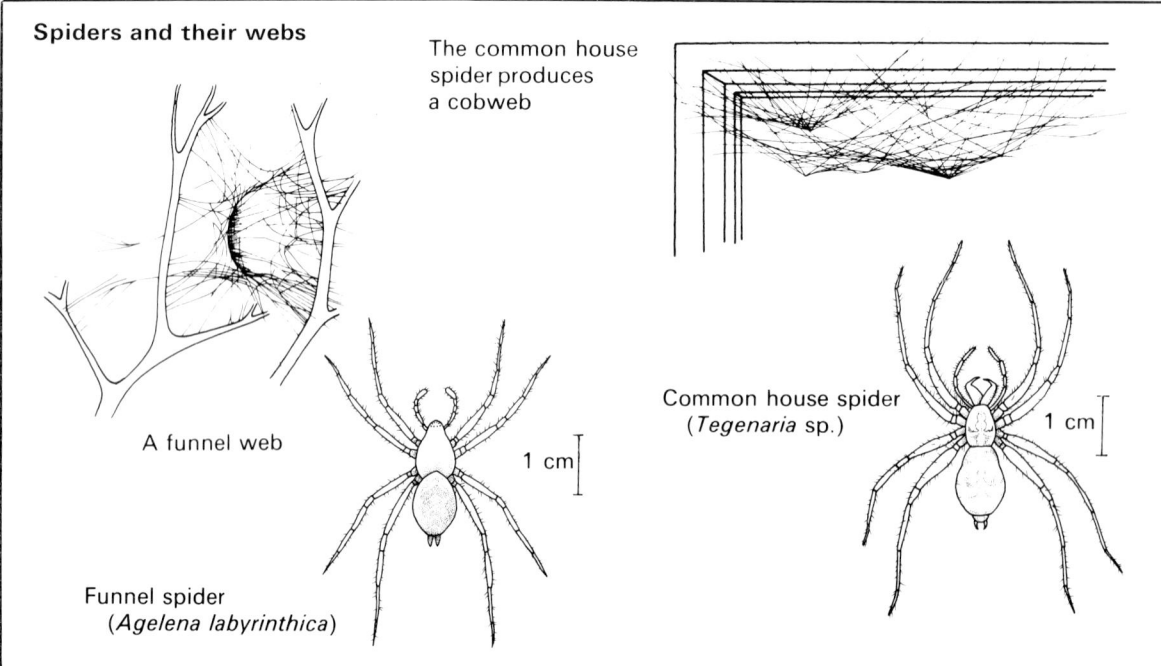

Spiders and their webs

The common house spider produces a cobweb

A funnel web

Funnel spider (*Agelena labyrinthica*)

Common house spider (*Tegenaria* sp.)

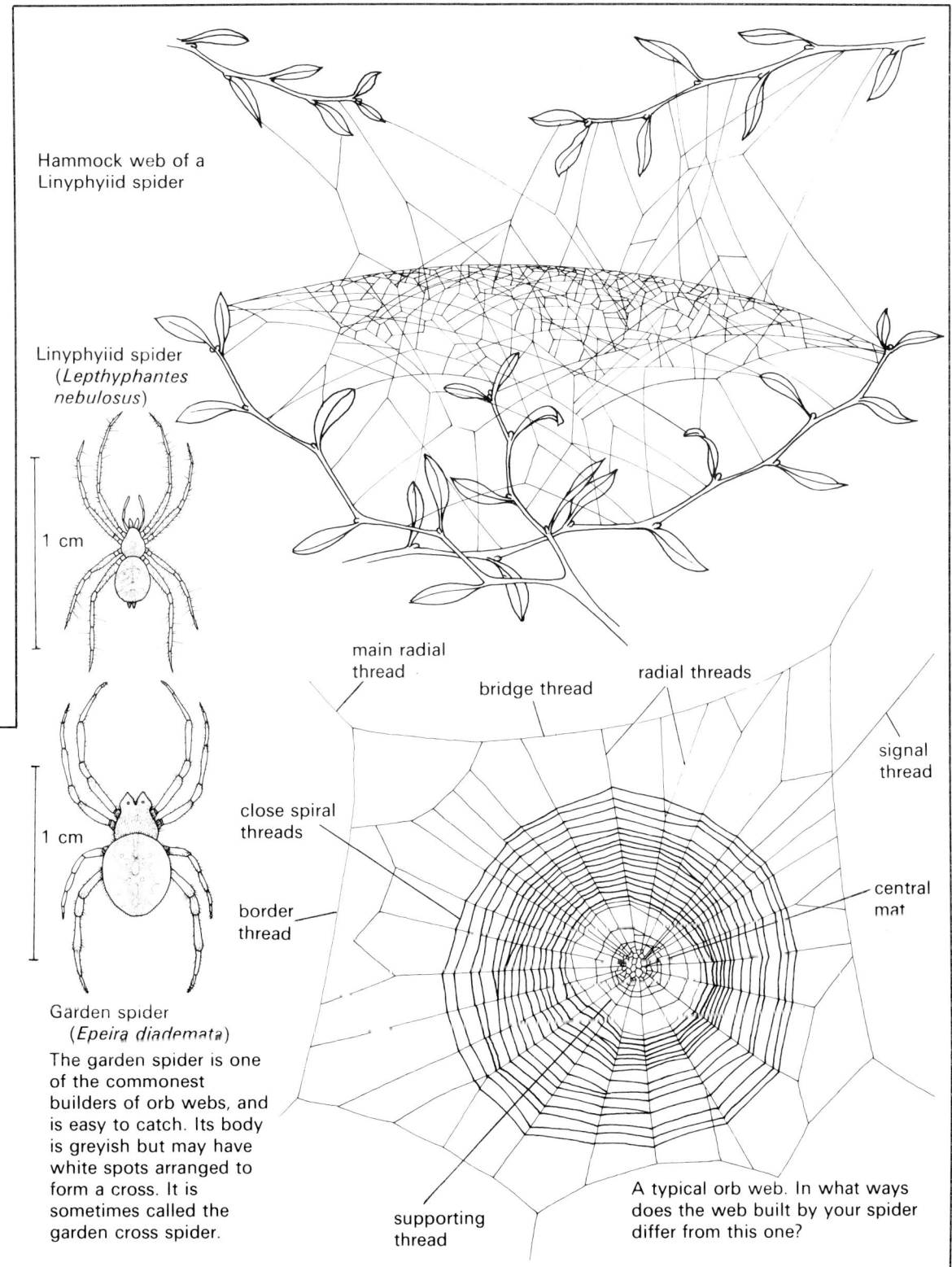

Hammock web of a Linyphyiid spider

Linyphyiid spider (*Lepthyphantes nebulosus*)

1 cm

1 cm

Garden spider (*Epeira diademata*)
The garden spider is one of the commonest builders of orb webs, and is easy to catch. Its body is greyish but may have white spots arranged to form a cross. It is sometimes called the garden cross spider.

main radial thread
bridge thread
radial threads
close spiral threads
signal thread
border thread
central mat
supporting thread

A typical orb web. In what ways does the web built by your spider differ from this one?

clockwise? Are the answers to the above questions always the same for the same spider? Are they the same for different spiders?

6 Spinning another spiral more closely spaced than the one it spins at first. How many turns has this one? Is it made from the inside outward or outside inward? What does it do with the first spiral (**5**) as it makes this new spiral.

7 Finally, it may spin a signal thread from the web (which part?) to its hiding place (where?)

Try making a series of drawings to show the stages of web-building by your spider. Note the time at which each drawing is made so you can find out how long the process takes. Some of the threads will have small drops of sticky fluid on them for trapping insects while some threads will have no stickiness. Find out which ones are sticky and which are not. Later, if you catch a spider of a different kind, you may find that its web-building habits are quite different.

The other main types of web are the shelf-like *cobweb*, built by the common house spider, the *funnel web* and the *hammock web*. Why does a cobweb have this name? Look for all these types of web and try to catch the spiders that build them so that you can watch the stages of web-building. Are the webs sticky or not? Throw some small insects into the web and find out what prevents them getting out before the spider can catch them.

Another investigation you can try is to destroy part of a web and then watch the spider repair it. Does it rebuild it exactly as it was?

FEEDING SPIDERS

Spiders can live for several days without food, but if you keep a spider for longer than a few days, you must feed it. Catch some flies, small moths, mosquitoes or other fairly small insects and keep them alive in a jar. To feed the spider, throw the insect into the web so that it is caught by the sticky threads. As it struggles to get free it shakes the web, arousing the spider who comes and investigates. Watch what the spider does with its trapped prey. The spider has fangs on the ends of its jaws and with these it paralyses the prey by injecting it with poisons. It then feeds on the prey by biting it with its jaws and sucking the body juices from it. Does your spider feed on the prey at once or does it wrap it in sticky threads and feed on it later? If it feeds later, how much later? How many insects does your spider feed on each day? If you give it more insects than it needs, what does it do with these extra insects?

TAKING A WEB

An orb web is more clearly seen if you 'take it' on to a wire loop. Make the loop just a little bigger than the outline of the web, place it behind the web, and then bring it towards you slowly so that the main radial threads all touch the wire at the same time. Move it further towards you so that the threads stick to the wire and break away from the support.

A more permanent way of taking a web is to use a piece of black cardboard with Copydex thinly smeared in a narrow band around the edges. Pick up the web on this card, as with the wire loop.

AFTERWARDS

When you have finished studying the web-building of your spider, release it in a place similar to that in which it was found.

The harvestman looks like a spider at first glance for it has eight legs, but its body is not divided into two parts by a narrow waist, as is the body of a spider.

2 A mini-aquarium

It is often a good idea to have several small aquaria instead of one larger one, as it is easier to see the animals and to study them when they are in a small volume of water: they cannot swim so far or so fast. With several separate aquaria, each kind of animal can be given the type of food it needs, and animals that feed on other animals can be kept apart.

You can keep your animals in jam jars, pickle jars, plastic sandwich boxes or many other kinds of ready-made container such as those in which ice-cream is sold. On the whole, shallow containers are better than deep ones. One of the cheapest ways of providing accommodation for lots of small water animals is to make your own mini-aquaria, as described below.

WHAT YOU NEED

A piece of thick, stiff cardboard about 40 cm × 15 cm for each tank—you could instead modify the design, using pieces of hardboard or preferably thin plywood, in which case you could make slightly larger aquaria; a roll of transparent plastic sandwich bags; one large, wide rubber band for each tank; Bostik or other glue suitable for gluing the cardboard—if you are using plywood or hardboard, use a wood glue and small panel pins to fix the sections together; a supply of jars or plastic containers with screw-on or snap-on lids.

A plankton net (see drawing) is very useful for catching very small animals in ponds or streams, and a *small* aquarium net is useful for transferring animals from one aquarium to another.

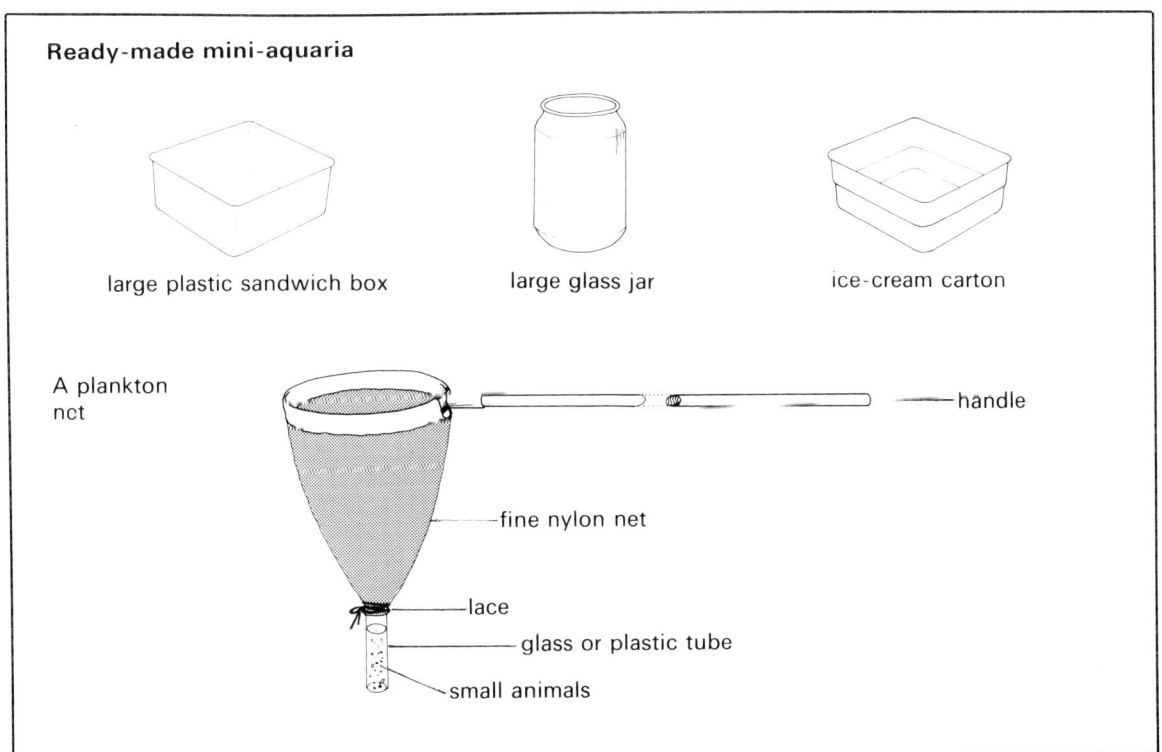

MAKING THE MINI-AQUARIUM

The design shown in the drawing is to be cut out of cardboard in one piece. Then it is folded round and glued, as shown, to make a frame. The width of each side of the frame should be a little less than half the width of your plastic bag. For example, if the bag measures 20 cm across, make each section about 9.5 cm wide. The frame will extend the bag almost fully but without overstretching it, and there will be enough slackness to allow the bag to be folded out over the top of the frame.

The height of the frame should be at least 2 cm less than the length of the bag so that the bottom of the bag will rest firmly on the surface on which the frame is standing. If you are using hardboard or plywood, cut each of the four sides separately and join them with glue and nails. Do not be tempted to make too large a frame from cardboard, unless it is very thick indeed. With most kinds of cardboard the greatest practicable size of frame is about 10 cm × 10 cm × 10 cm.

The bag is fixed to the frame by simply folding the edge of the bag out over the top of the frame and securing it with a large rubber band.

To cover the aquarium, use a square of acetate film or thin glass.

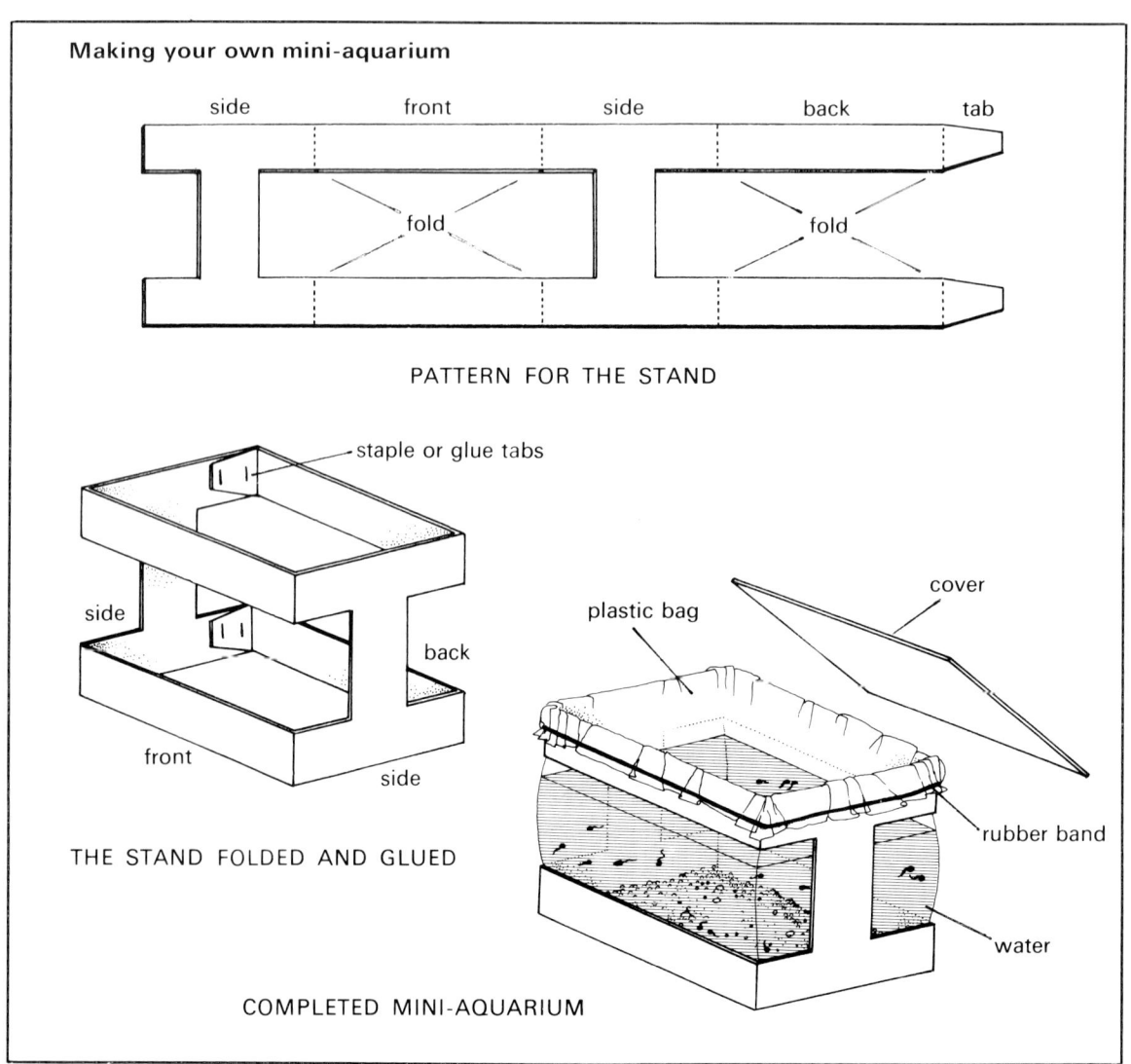

SETTING UP A MINI-AQUARIUM

Fill the aquarium *to the brim* with water and leave it overnight on the sink draining-board to check that there are no leaks in the bag. It will not be filled as full later so if it can withstand the water pressure when full, it will be safe. At the same time as you fill the aquarium, put some tap-water into a clean shallow dish to stand overnight.

If there are no leaks, put the aquarium in an undisturbed place. A good position is the sill of a northfacing window where the plants in the aquarium will receive light, but not direct sunlight.

If the bag has developed no leaks, empty the water out of the aquarium into another container. In the bottom of the bag place some pond-mud, some fine washed gravel or some washed sand—the layer should be about 2 cm deep. Now pour in the water that has stood overnight. The water level should be between half-way and two-thirds of the way up the aquarium. If you have put mud in the aquarium, leave it to stand for several hours, or perhaps overnight, for this to settle. Washed sand or gravel should settle immediately, but these have the disadvantage that they do not provide mineral nutrients for the plants.

PLANTS FOR THE AQUARIUM

You can get these from a pond or river (if you ask the landowner first), or buy them from your local aquarist's shop. One of the easiest plants to grow is Canadian Pondweed (*Elodea*). Duckweed (*Lemna*) is common in ponds but is not usually sold in shops. A few small plants will help provide shade and shelter for the animals, and food for some of them. The submerged plants produce oxygen which dissolves in the water, keeping it well aerated.

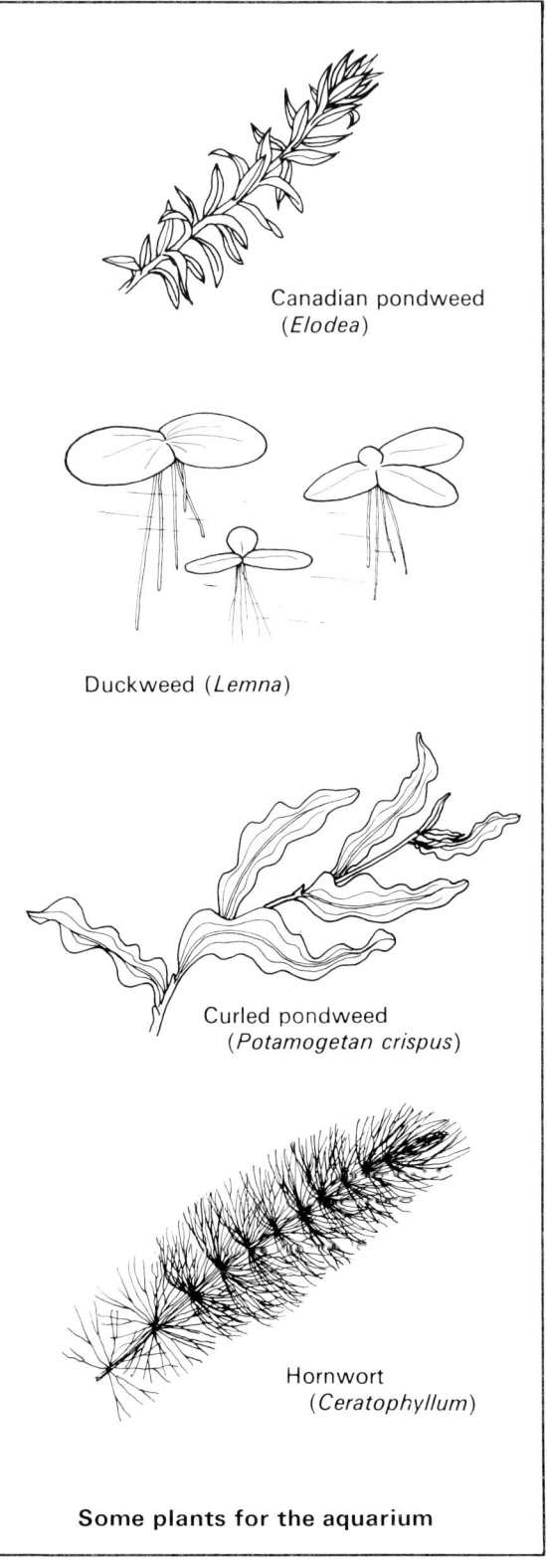

Canadian pondweed (*Elodea*)

Duckweed (*Lemna*)

Curled pondweed (*Potamogetan crispus*)

Hornwort (*Ceratophyllum*)

Some plants for the aquarium

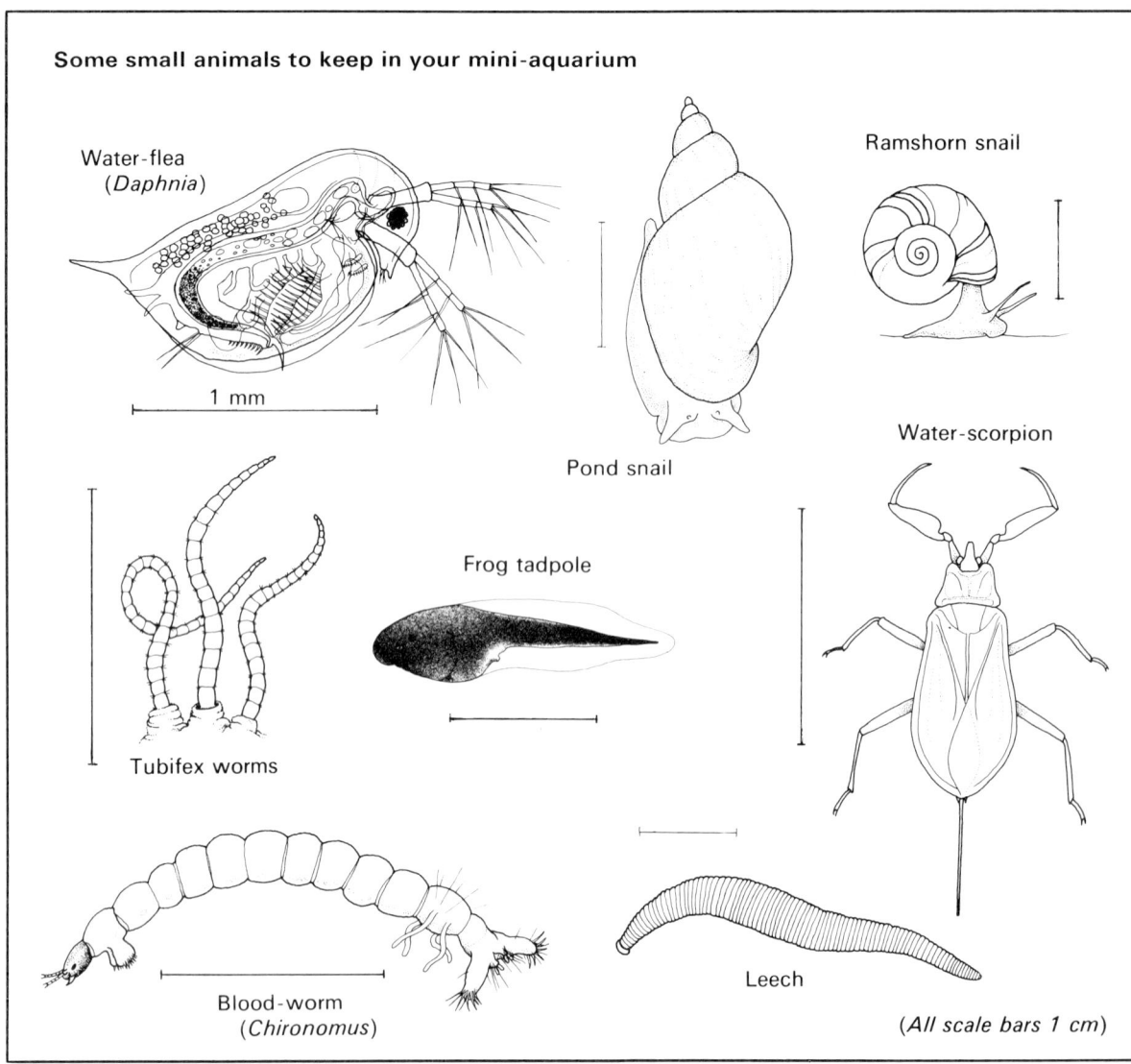

Some small animals to keep in your mini-aquarium

(*All scale bars 1 cm*)

ANIMALS FOR THE AQUARIUM

The drawings show a few of the many dozens of different kinds of animals that are easy to keep in a small aquarium, for a short while, at least.

Water-fleas (*Daphnia*), blood-worms and a few other kinds of small animal can be purchased cheaply from aquarists' shops, where they are sold as live food for tropical fish. Water-fleas and many similar animals can be fed on even smaller water animals (see Chapter 5). Alternatively, they can be fed by adding a small pinch of malted milk powder (e.g. Horlicks) to the water every day.

To keep Tubifex worms, the aquarium must have a layer of mud on the bottom and a supply of fresh-water continuously dripping into the aquarium. If you buy water plants from an aquarist's shop, you will often find small animals on them, especially water-snails. These can be kept for a long time and are likely to breed. Water-snails feed on the green growth (algae) that gradually covers the inside of the aquarium and the stones at the bottom. If the aquarium is in bright light (though not *direct* sunlight), the growth of algae will be encouraged, and this will provide ample food for the snails. The same applies to the snails you may catch in a pond.

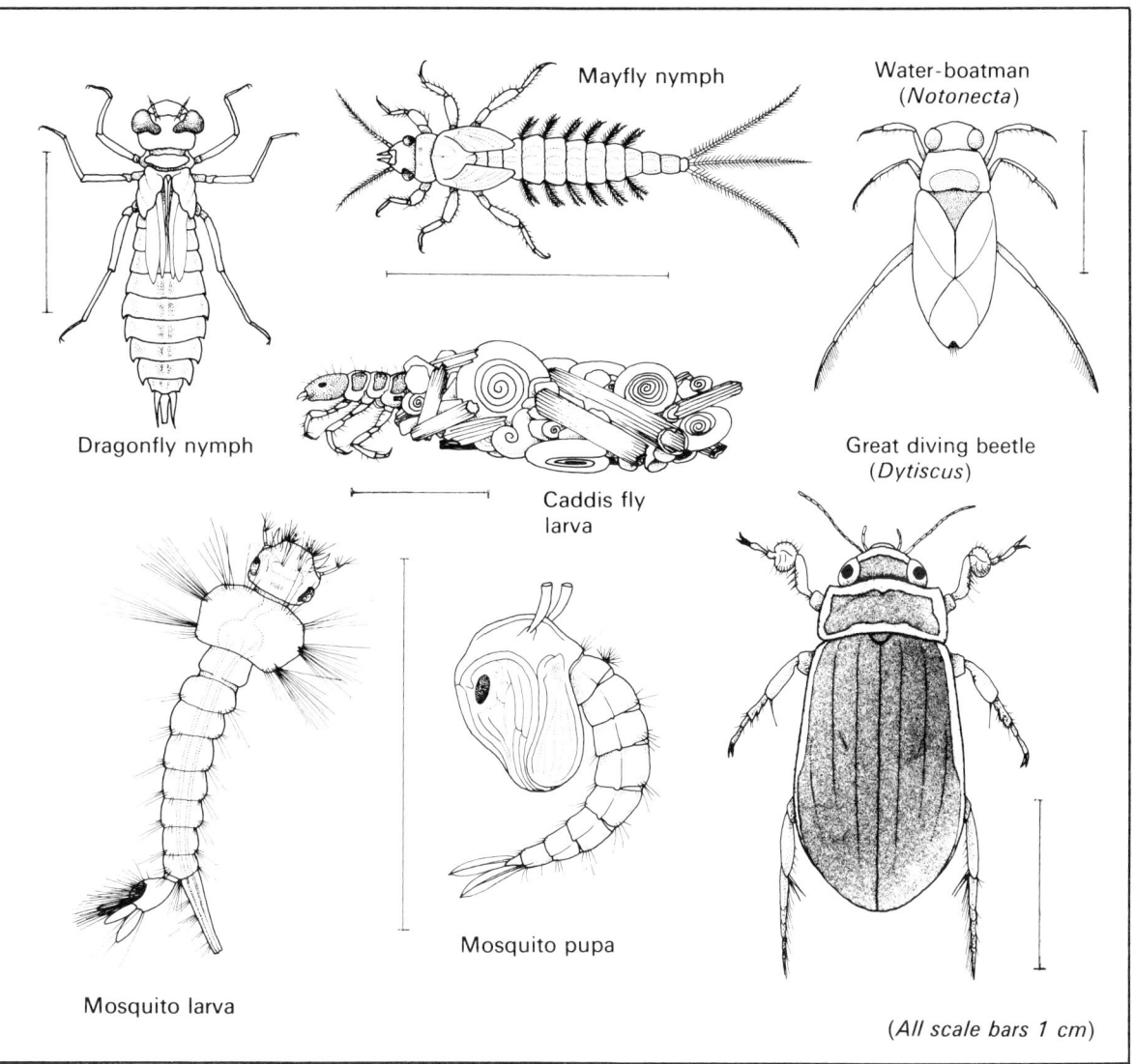

(All scale bars 1 cm)

Use the plankton net or a fine kitchen sieve (see drawing) to catch animals swimming in midwater. When you hold the net up to drain, the small animals will have been collected in the glass tube, which you can then tip into a jar. Another good way of obtaining animals from a pond is to scoop up the surface layers of soft mud from the bottom—use the net (carefully!), a small shovel or a large spoon. Spread out the mud and water in a shallow dish, and examine it. You will often find nymphs of dragonflies and mayflies as well as caddis fly larvae. Dragonfly nymphs, waterboatmen and the great diving beetle (*Dytiscus*) are carnivores. Keep these in separate aquaria, otherwise they will eat each other. Feed them by hanging a piece of raw meat (or chopped worm) on a length of thread. They are more likely to 'attack' it if you move it around in the water. Do not leave the meat in the water for more than an hour or two, for it will soon begin to decay and pollute the water. They can also be fed on live maggots (buy from a fishing tackle shop as live bait). The dragonfly nymphs may take up to 2 years before they moult into the adult form.

When you are catching pond animals, take some of the pondweed and the stems of plants growing half-submerged at the water's edge too. Put these

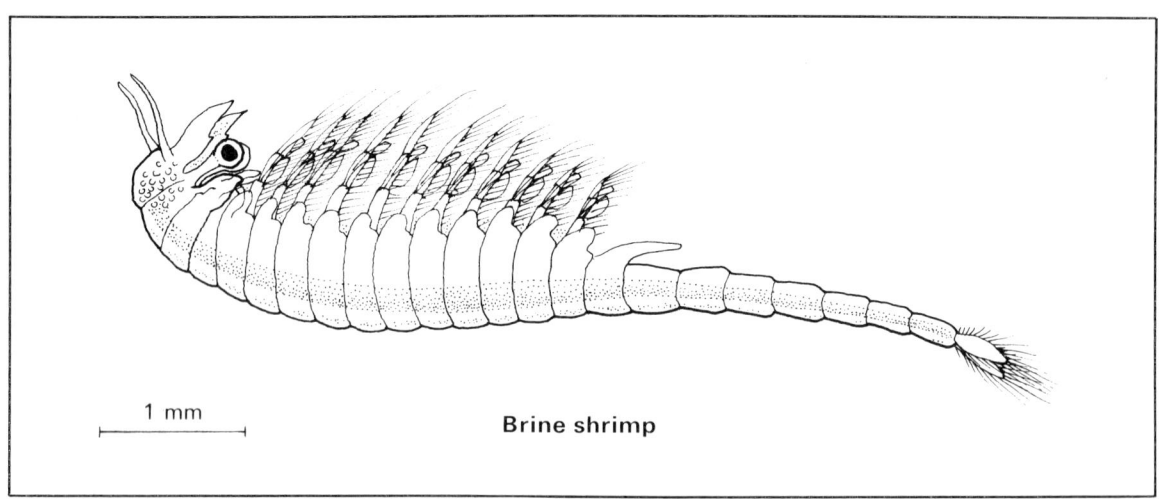

1 mm
Brine shrimp

in a shallow dish and look for small animals on the stems and on the underside of leaves.

If you live in a low-lying area where there are ponds and canals, there may be plenty of mosquitoes and gnats around in summer. These will visit your aquarium and lay their eggs there if you leave the aquarium uncovered. You can then watch them go through their larval and pupal stages before finally hatching out as adults. As larvae they feed on microscopic water animals (see Chapter 5).

Brine shrimps are bought as brine shrimps eggs from an aquarist's shop. A small tube contains tens of thousands of eggs. Put enough eggs to cover a ½p piece in a small container of *salt* solution. The exact strength of solution does not matter—about 1 dessertspoonful of cooking salt in 1 litre of tap-water is suitable. The eggs need to be put in a warm place to hatch. In summer, put them in a greenhouse (shaded from the sun) or in a warm corner outdoors. In winter, put them in the airing cupboard. An electric yoghurt-maker is also a good place in which to hatch the eggs. In 2 days they will have hatched and can be transferred to the aquarium (containing a salt solution) where they can be kept at room temperature like water-fleas. As they do best if the water is aerated only half fill the aquarium. If you have an aquarium aerator, or can use a bicycle pump to bubble air through the water several times daily, you can fill the tank more than half-full. Brine shrimps can be fed by mixing a few dozen 'grains' of dried baking yeast (or a tiny piece of fresh yeast) gently with water and making a paste, which is then added to the water in the aquarium. Do not give *too much* food. If the food you have given is not completely eaten, or if the water becomes cloudy, stop feeding the shrimps for a few days. The brine shrimps will grow during the course of the next 5 to 6 weeks, becoming up to 1 cm long.

With good care and feeding, the small animals can live for several weeks in the mini-aquarium—maybe even longer. If they do not seem to be doing too well, or if you have seen all you want to see, let the collected animals free again in the pond or other place from which you first took them.

3 Collecting galls

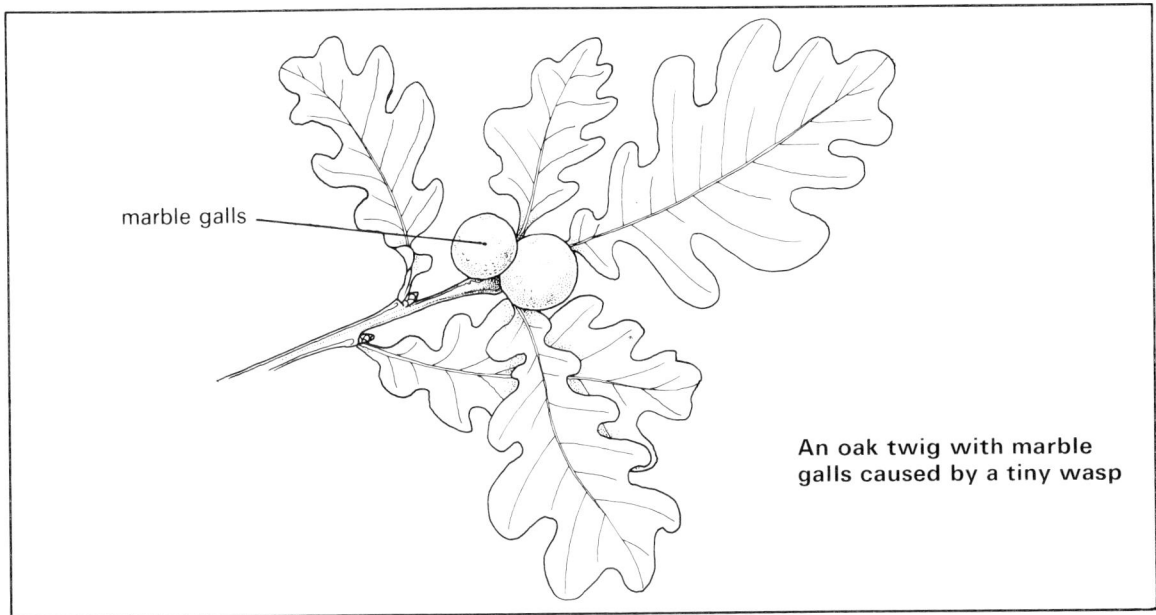

An oak twig with marble galls caused by a tiny wasp

Many kinds of insect lay their eggs inside the leaves of plants. Others lay them in the stems, in the roots or in buds. The eggs hatch into small maggot-like larvae that feed on the plant from the inside. Often, the affected part of the plant becomes badly damaged and it finally dies.

Some plants have developed a method of defence against this kind of attack. As soon as an egg is laid the plant begins to grow rapidly in the region around the egg, forming a swelling, which is called a *gall*. The egg hatches inside the gall, and the larva feeds and grows there without entering the other parts of the plant. In this way the plant provides the larva with somewhere to live and feed, but keeps it in one place where it cannot damage the leaves, buds or other important parts of the plant.

Later, when the larva is fully grown, it becomes a pupa. After a while the skin of the pupa splits open, and the fully-formed adult insect (or *imago*) emerges and tunnels its way out of the gall. It flies away, usually to mate, and the females lay eggs on fresh plants to begin the cycle all over again.

Only certain types of insect and plant show such characteristics. Different types of gall are produced by each insect–plant pair, as you can see in the drawings on the following pages.

WHAT YOU NEED

A number of small jars (jam jars, pickle jars) or plastic containers (such as yoghurt containers); a roll of transparent plastic bags (large size); a supply of large rubber bands; some ice-cream cartons; thin garden canes; cotton-wool; paper tissues; a small jar of water to take with you when you are collecting; potting compost or well-rotted garden compost mixed with soil.

You will also need the usual collecting equipment such as a knife (or scalpel) and scissors for removing gall-bearing parts from plants. A pair of secateurs might also be useful.

WHAT TO DO

One of the best plants to examine for galls is an oak tree. For preference, choose one that is on its own in a hedgerow rather than one in a wood with many other trees, as single trees tend to have more galls on them.

The drawings show some galls to look for.

It is best to look for galls on oak in April or May. By June or July the insect may have gone. A hole shows where an insect has left a gall. Galls of various types can be found on other plants all through the spring and summer and even into early autumn, so *any* time of the year except winter is suitable for gall-hunting. When you have found the galls you must decide whether they are newly formed and still growing (this is most likely in spring), or whether their growth is complete.

If they are still growing, it is best to leave them on the plant. Make a note of their position and come back a few weeks later to collect them when they are fully grown. You could take home just a few to cut open and look for the young larva or larvae, as in some types of gall there is always more than one larva, each in its own separate section.

If the galls are fully grown, cut off the twig or stem and wrap its cut end in cotton-wool or paper tissue that has been soaked in water. Then seal it in a plastic bag to take home. If you find galls on garden weeds you can use a trowel to transfer the plant to a pot of soil. At home, place the plant in a cage, made like the one in the drawing. You could use just two canes if you prefer. Make sure that there are no small cracks or openings through which the emerging adult insect can escape. Remember that most adult gall insects are only a few millimetres long and *only one or two millimetres wide*. If a lot of moisture collects inside the bag, wipe it off, looking

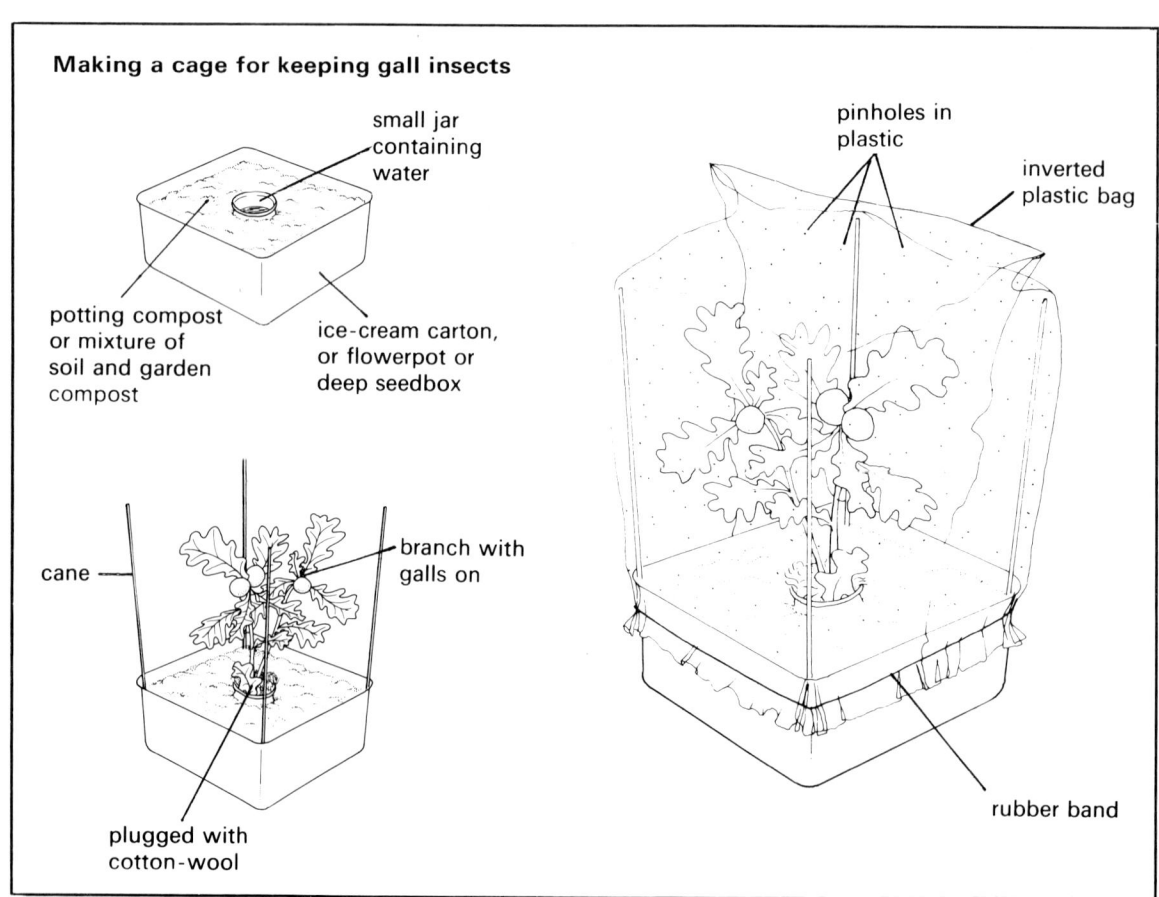

Making a cage for keeping gall insects

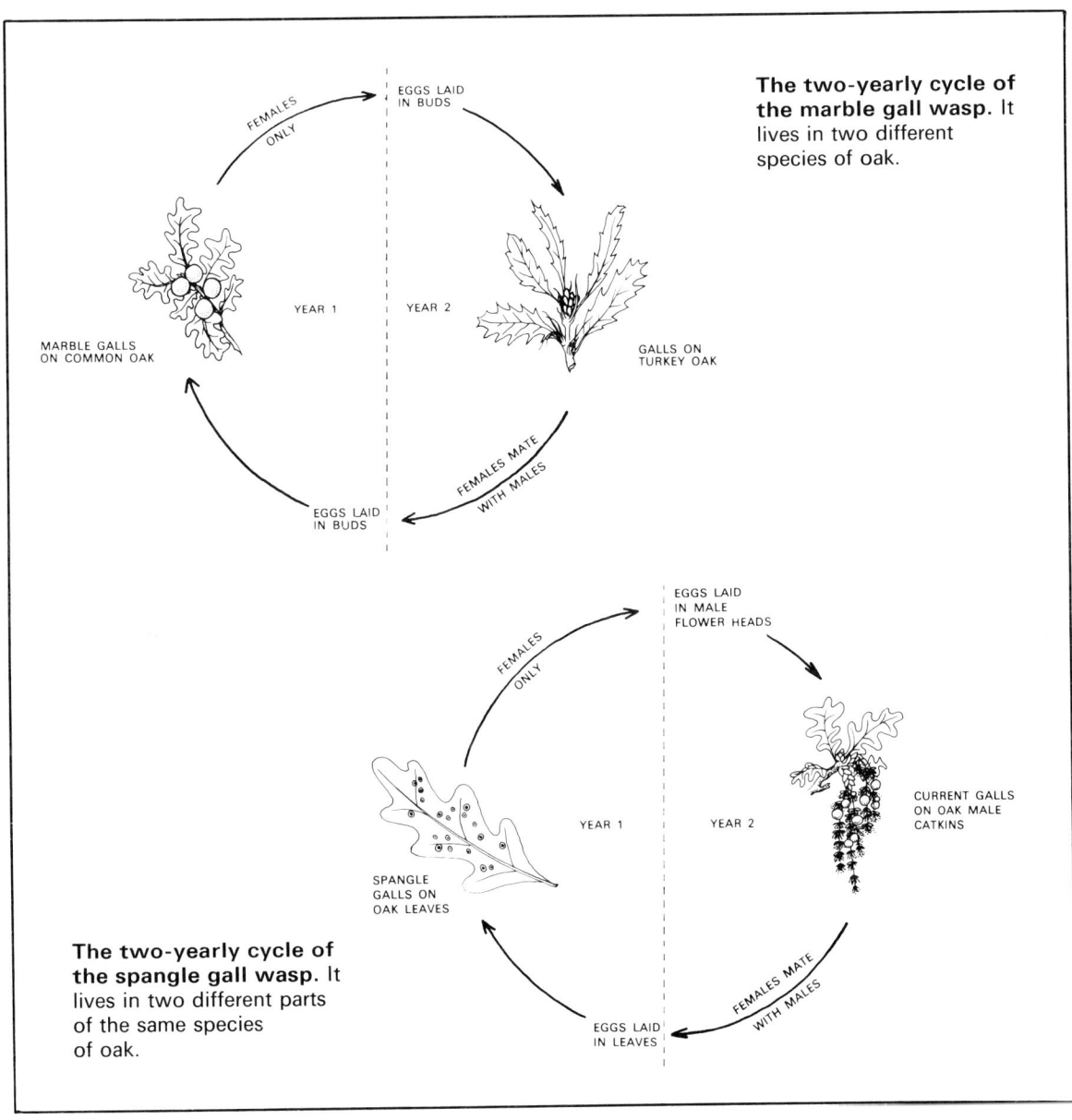

The two-yearly cycle of the marble gall wasp. It lives in two different species of oak.

The two-yearly cycle of the spangle gall wasp. It lives in two different parts of the same species of oak.

carefully for adult insects as you do so. Turn the bag inside out, shake off the surplus moisture and replace the bag inside-out on the canes. This takes only a few minutes and should be done every few days. Occasionally, you may need to top up the water and to water the compost to keep it *just* damp.

FOLLOWING THE LIFE-CYCLE
If you find the galls early enough, cut open one gall each week to follow the stages in the development of the insect. Make a *small* cut and then try to pull the gall to pieces bit by bit. In this way you are more likely to extract the whole larva without damaging it. Make sketches of the larva or pupa, remembering to write the date in each drawing. It is best if you make each drawing to the same scale. The complete set of drawings will show how much the larva grows. Often, you may find larvae of other kinds of insect sharing the same gall. These are called *inquilines* and do not harm the gall insect larva. Keep most of the

galls intact so that the larvae can develop undisturbed. Sooner or later you will find one or more adult insects crawling around inside the cage. When you have studied the adult, let it go—unless you intend to study the mating (see previous page). If you have several galls, more adults should emerge in the course of the next week or two, some of which may be the adults of inquiline insects. If the galls normally have only one insect inside each, count how many adults you have collected altogether. Is this number equal to the number of galls? If not, it probably means that some of the larvae have become victims of certain flies that lay eggs inside them. The larvae of such flies are *parasites* that feed on and finally kill the larva or pupa of the gall insect.

If you notice several exit holes in the galls but have found no adults, it is possible that the larvae have crawled down into the compost or soil before becoming pupae. This is the habit of a few of the gall-causing insects. Wait a while longer for the adult insects to hatch and come up out of the soil.

THE NEXT STAGE

As the adults appear, transfer them to a cage such as that described on p. 33. You will need to put fine netting over the cage to prevent the insects escaping. The cage should contain fresh twigs or shoots of the plant on which the insect lays its eggs, but more about this later. If you watch carefully you *may* also be lucky enough to see the male and female adults mating or to see the females laying their eggs. Do not be disappointed if you do not see anything of either of these events. Many kinds of gall insect produce two types of gall, which are found on two kinds of plant. (The drawings show some examples of this.) If you hatch adults from *one* kind of plant they need plants of the *other* type to lay their eggs on. Another reason why you may not see them mating is that some adults can lay eggs without mating first. If you become keen on following the life-cycle of gall insects, useful reference books are *The Pocket Encyclopaedia of Plant Galls* by Arnold Darlington (Blandford Press) and *The World of a Tree* by Arnold Darlington (Faber and Faber).

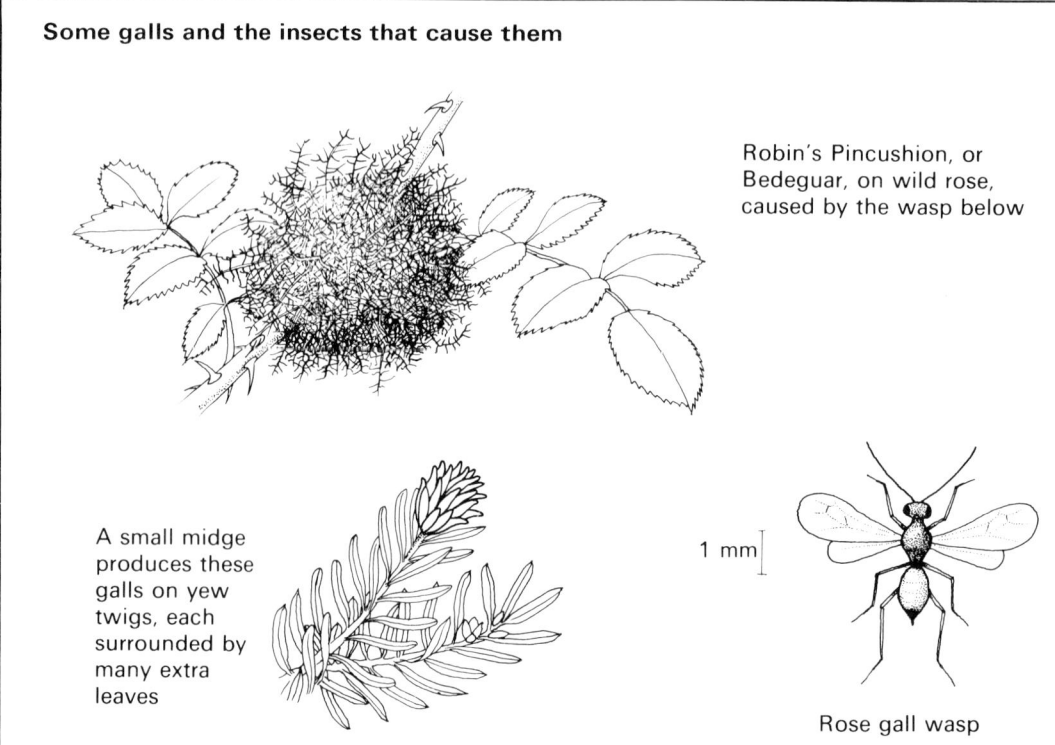

Some galls and the insects that cause them

Robin's Pincushion, or Bedeguar, on wild rose, caused by the wasp below

A small midge produces these galls on yew twigs, each surrounded by many extra leaves

1 mm

Rose gall wasp

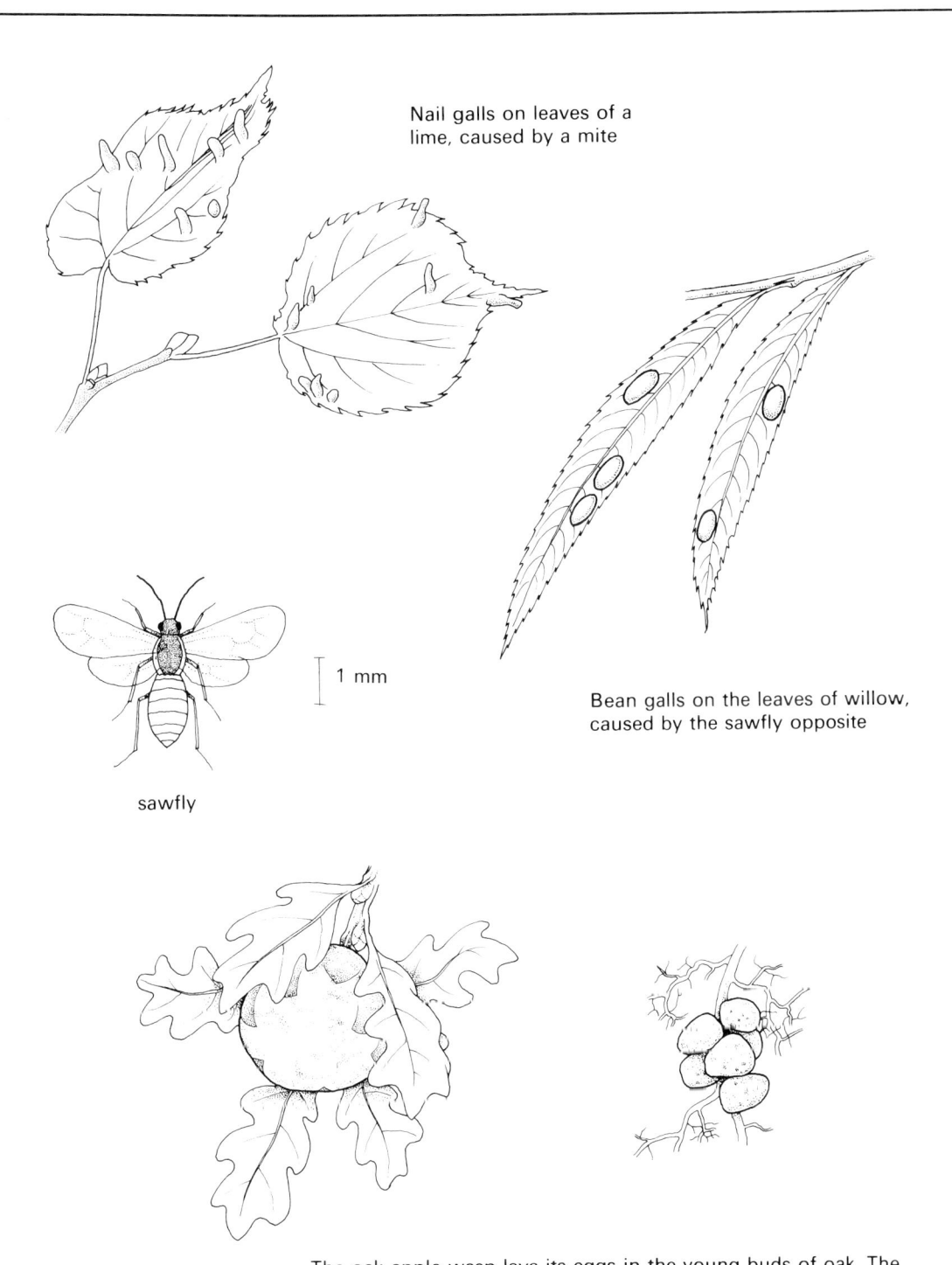

Nail galls on leaves of a lime, caused by a mite

1 mm

sawfly

Bean galls on the leaves of willow, caused by the sawfly opposite

The oak apple wasp lays its eggs in the young buds of oak. The hatched males and females mate, then the females lay eggs in the roots of the tree, producing root galls

4 The life of aphids

Aphids, often known as greenfly or blackfly, are very common insects. You will have no difficulty in finding some for this project. One reason for them being so common is that they reproduce at a high rate, and their high reproduction rate is one of the main topics of this chapter.

The life of aphids has some interesting features, as the drawing shows. Females hatch from eggs in the spring and then fly away to find new plants to feed on. They feed by pushing their mouth parts, which form a fine needle-like tube, into the tissues of the plants. Then they suck the nourishing juices from the plant. Soon they begin to multiply, but not by mating and laying eggs. These females do not lay eggs; they give birth to young aphids, all of which are females. Some of these have wings and fly away to start new colonies of aphids on other plants. Most have no wings but stay on the same plant, feeding and multiplying. Towards the end of the summer both female and male aphids are produced, all with wings. These mate, fly away and the females find new plants to lay eggs on. Often, the aphids feed on one kind of plant in spring and summer, but their eggs are laid on a different kind of plant.

Although these insects are often called greenfly or blackfly they do not belong among the true flies (*Diptera*). For instance, the true flies have one pair of wings while winged aphids have two pairs. Aphids belong to the insect group called *Hemiptera*, often known as 'bugs'. This group also includes water-stick insects, water-boatmen and frog hoppers (e.g. the 'cuckoo-spit' insect).

WHAT YOU NEED

One or more insect cages of the type described in Chapter 1; a medium-sized water-colour paintbrush. If you are studying the bean aphid (blackfly), you will need a packet of broad bean seeds and some seed trays or large flowerpots for growing a steady supply of food plants.

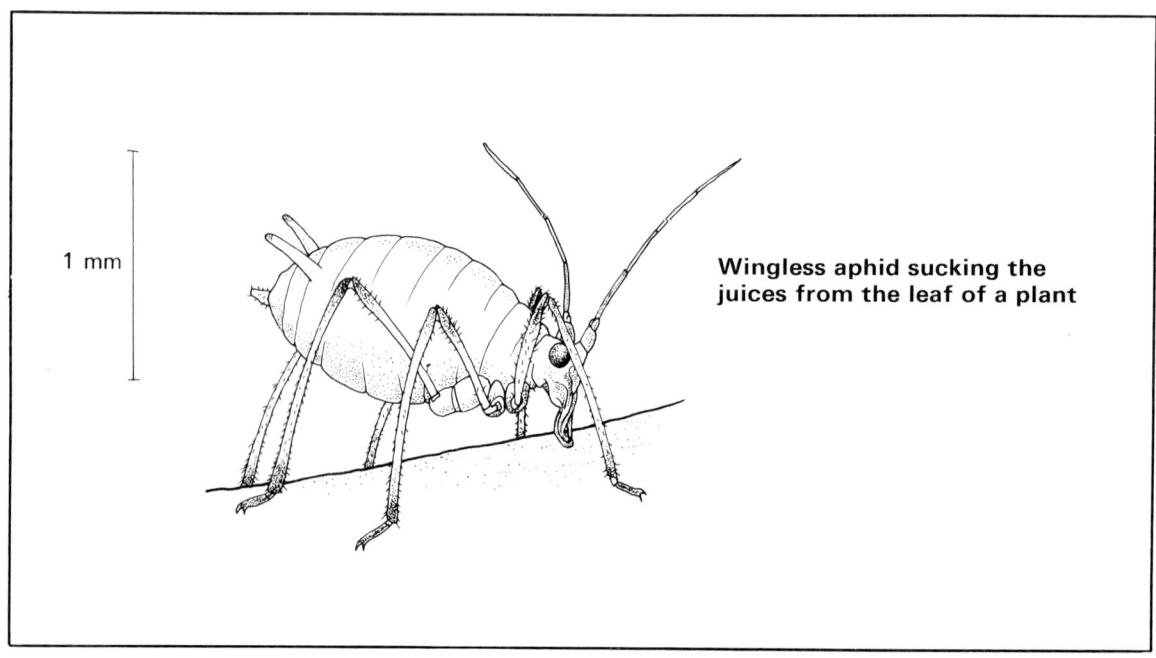

Wingless aphid sucking the juices from the leaf of a plant

1 mm

GETTING STARTED

This project is best begun in spring or early summer when the aphids first appear. May, June and July are the best months. Look for the aphids on young shoots of sycamore, oak, rose (wild or cultivated), apple or hawthorn. You may also find them on other kinds of plant. If you are beginning this project later in the year, look on cabbages and similar plants.

Collect just a few (between 1 and 5) aphids from one plant. To pick them up, moisten the paintbrush slightly, draw out the bristles to make a fine point and pick up the aphids with the tip of the brush. Transfer them to a small tube or box containing a few leaves from the same plant and take them home. Take with you a fresh shoot from the same kind of plant which has *no* aphids on it.

Put the shoot in the cage (p. 3) and gently place the aphids on it. Make a note of the date and the number of aphids.

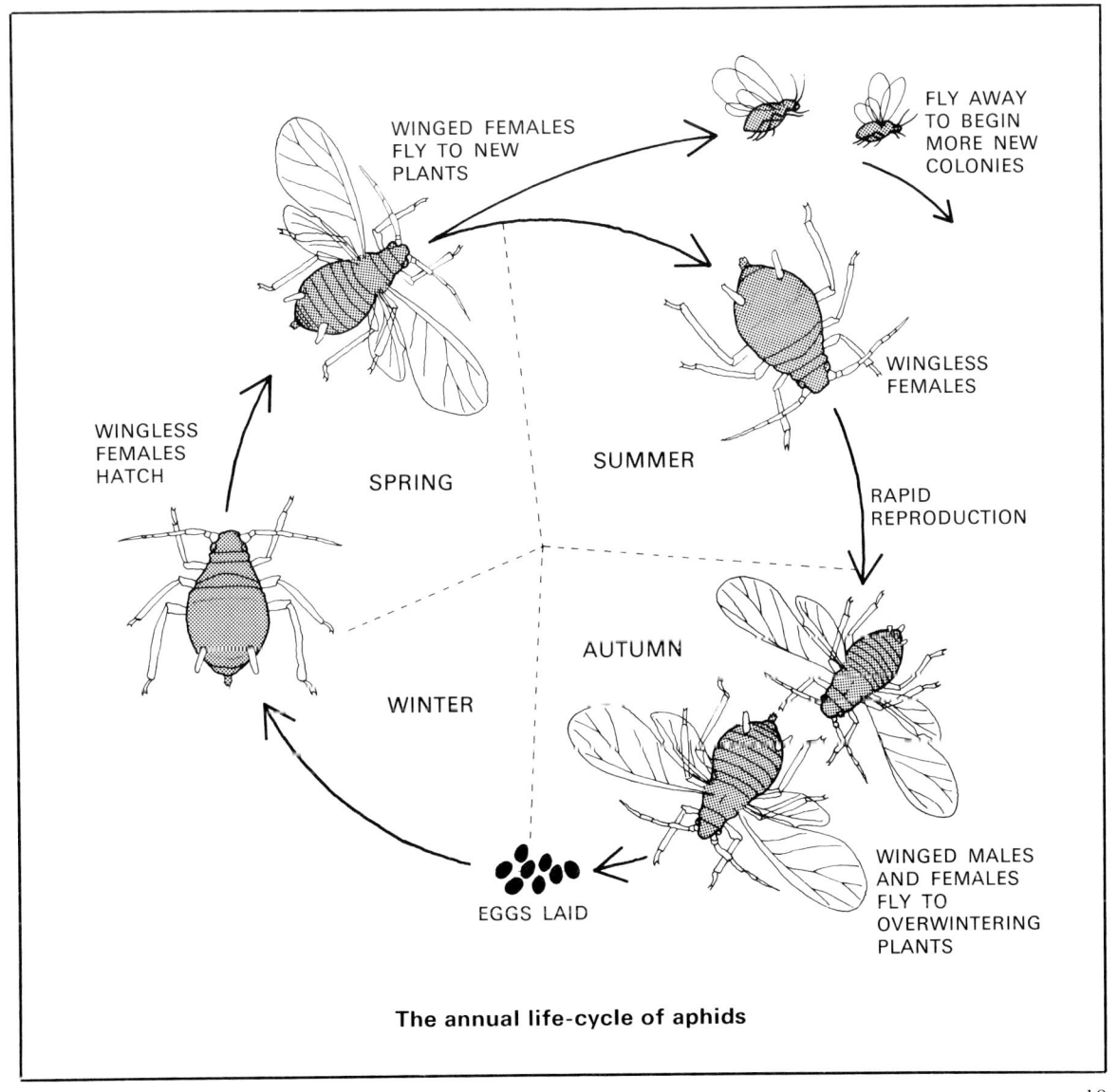

The annual life-cycle of aphids

KEEPING THE COLONY

On the same day each week, note the number of aphids on the plant. At the same time top up the water and, if necessary, replace the shoot with a fresh shoot of the same kind. Put the new shoot in the jar, close beside the old one, and after a day or so most of the aphids will have left the old shoot. Use the brush to transfer those that remain and then remove the old shoot.

WATCHING THE APHIDS

The aphids are wingless so it is safe to take the shoot out of the cage and watch the aphids. Use a hand-lens to see how they feed. Where do they feed?——on stems? on young leaves? on old leaves? on leaves of all ages? Does their feeding have any effect on the stem or leaf? You may be lucky enough to be watching when young aphids are born. If you are keeping ants (Chapter 12), put a stem or leaf bearing aphids in the ants' feeding compartment. The ants like to feed on the sugary liquid which the aphids produce in large drops from their rear end.

POPULATIONS

Your weekly counts of the numbers will make an interesting graph. Draw a graph similar to the one in the drawing.

You could also calculate the *increase* in the numbers each week. For example, if there were 25 aphids at the beginning of a week and there were 40 at the end, the increase is 25 → 40 = 15 aphids. Put this as a percentage of the number of aphids present at the beginning of the week:

$$\frac{\text{increase} \times 100}{\text{number at beginning}}\% = \frac{15 \times 100}{25}\% = 60\% \text{ increase}$$

Work out the percentage increase every week.

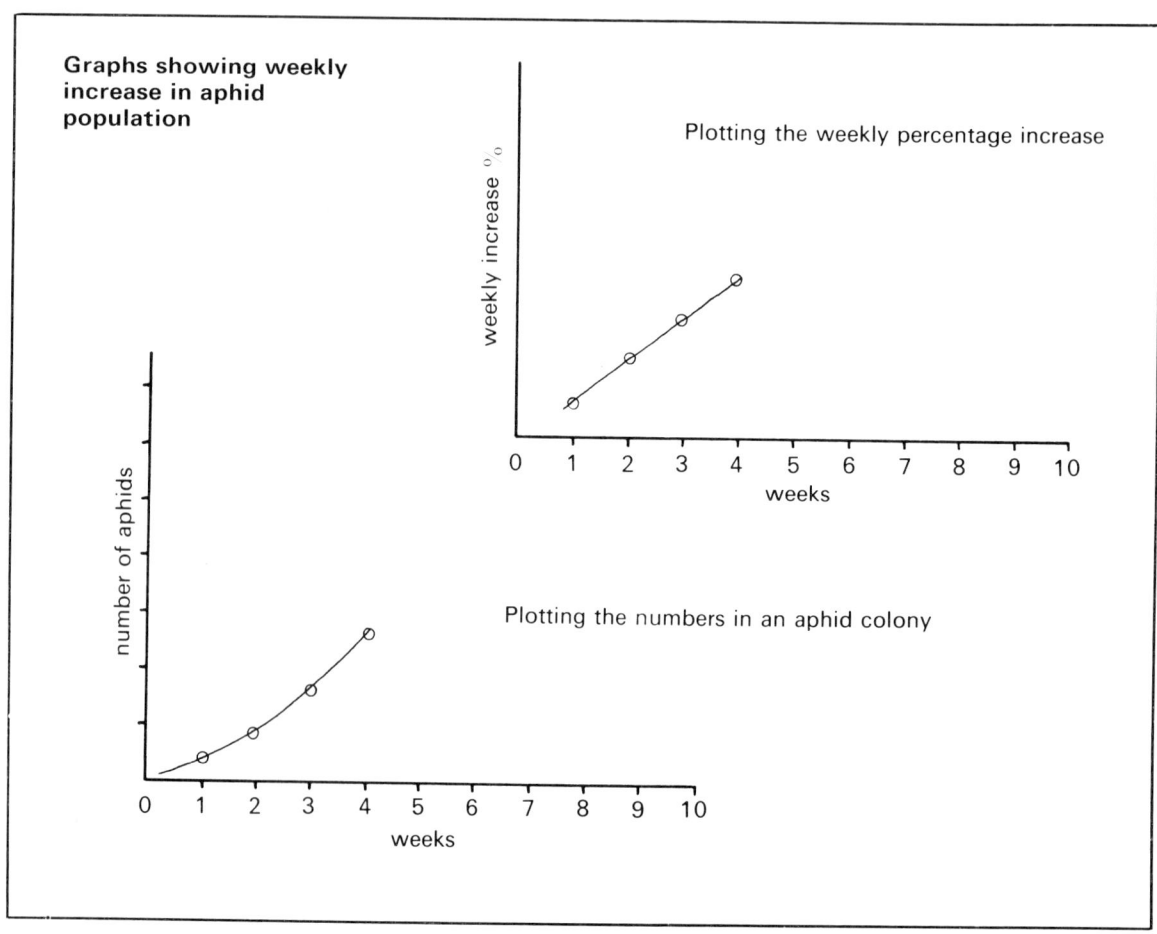

Graphs showing weekly increase in aphid population

Plotting the weekly percentage increase

Plotting the numbers in an aphid colony

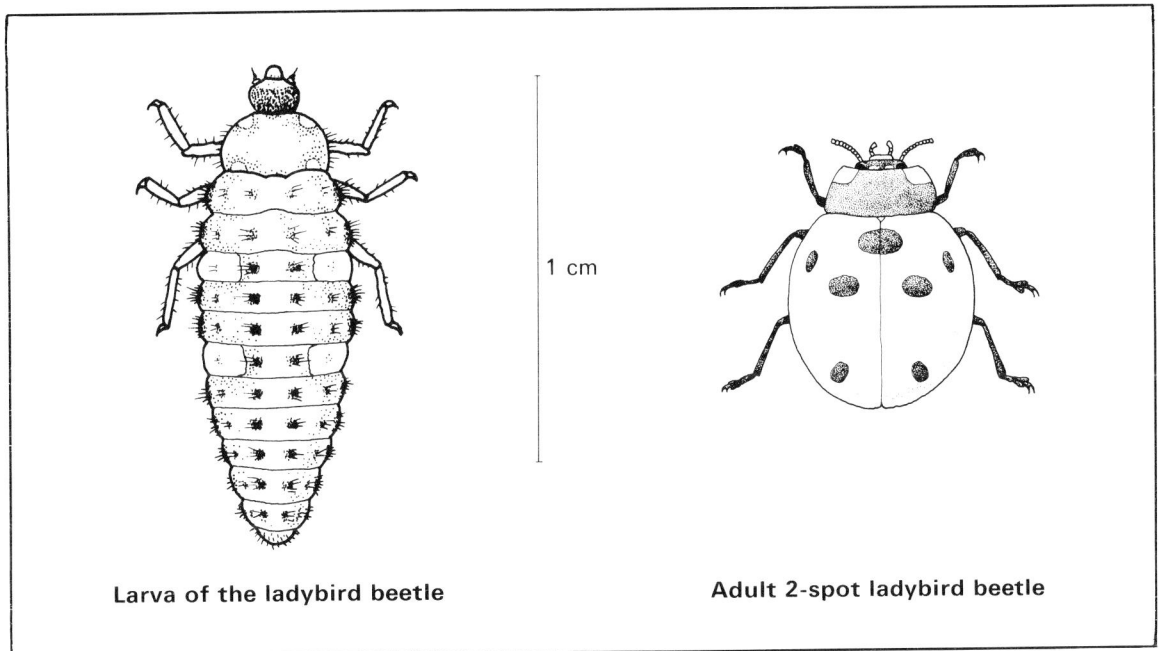

Larva of the ladybird beetle   Adult 2-spot ladybird beetle

What is the greatest percentage you find? At what date is the increase greatest? If one aphid multiplied at this rate for 1 year (52 weeks) how many aphids would be produced?

If you are keeping several different types of aphid you can work out the figure for each type separately and compare them.

PREDATORS

The population of aphids is normally kept down by other animals that feed on them. These include birds such as tits, the larvae of certain kinds of hover-fly, lace-wing flies and ladybird beetles (both adults and larvae). The newly-hatched ladybird larvae also feeds on aphid eggs. Try to catch a dozen or so adult ladybirds or larvae and place them in your aphid cage. Ladybird larvae can usually be found on plants where aphids are plentiful, for the adults tend to lay their eggs in such places. Find out if the predators prevent the number of aphids from increasing.

5 A water-drop microscope

Using ready-to-hand household materials this microscope costs almost nothing to make, yet it will help you to see dozens of different kinds of small animals.

WHAT YOU NEED

Some thin sheet aluminium (cut from a used drinks can); a small box or block of wood (*about*

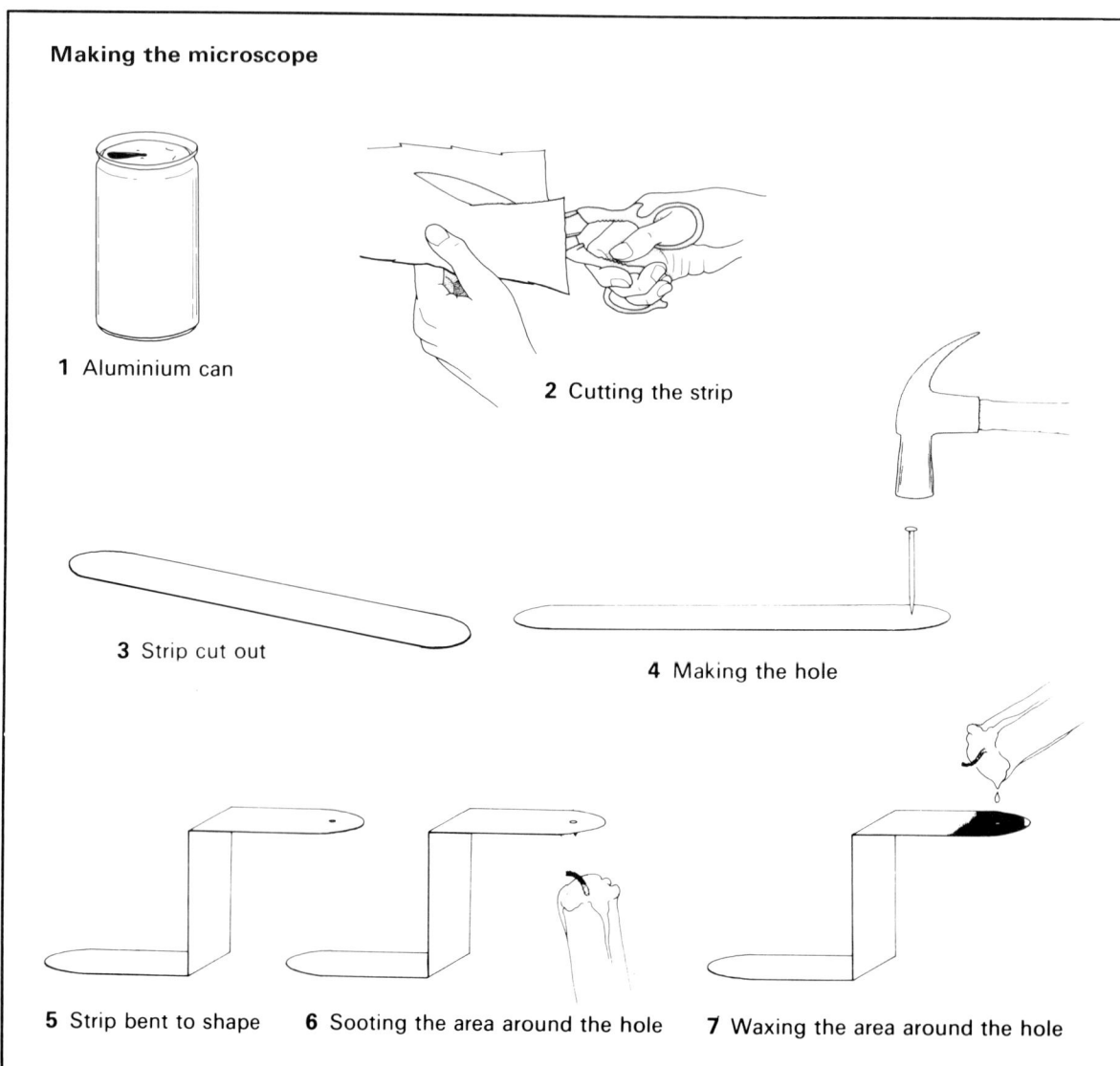

Making the microscope

1 Aluminium can

2 Cutting the strip

3 Strip cut out

4 Making the hole

5 Strip bent to shape

6 Sooting the area around the hole

7 Waxing the area around the hole

4 cm × 4 cm × 4 cm); two rubber bands; a candle; a hammer and a nail; tin-snips or strong scissors.

GETTING STARTED

First, cut out a strip of aluminium about 1 cm × 10 cm: the exact size does not matter. If the strip becomes curled when you cut it, put it on a hard flat surface and hammer it flat. Next, use the nail to make a hole near one end—the hole must not be too large. A single gentle tap with the hammer will force the point of the nail *partly* through the aluminium and will probably make a hole that is large enough. If the hole is too small, you can always enlarge it later. Finally, bend the strip as shown in the drawing.

Light the candle and hold the pierced end of the strip in the flame. Put it well into the lower part of the flame so that soot is deposited on both sides of the strip. Only the area around the hole needs to be sooted. Put the strip on a piece of folded newspaper or paper tissue, but first make sure that there is no chance of the hot strip damaging the table. Before the strip cools, take the

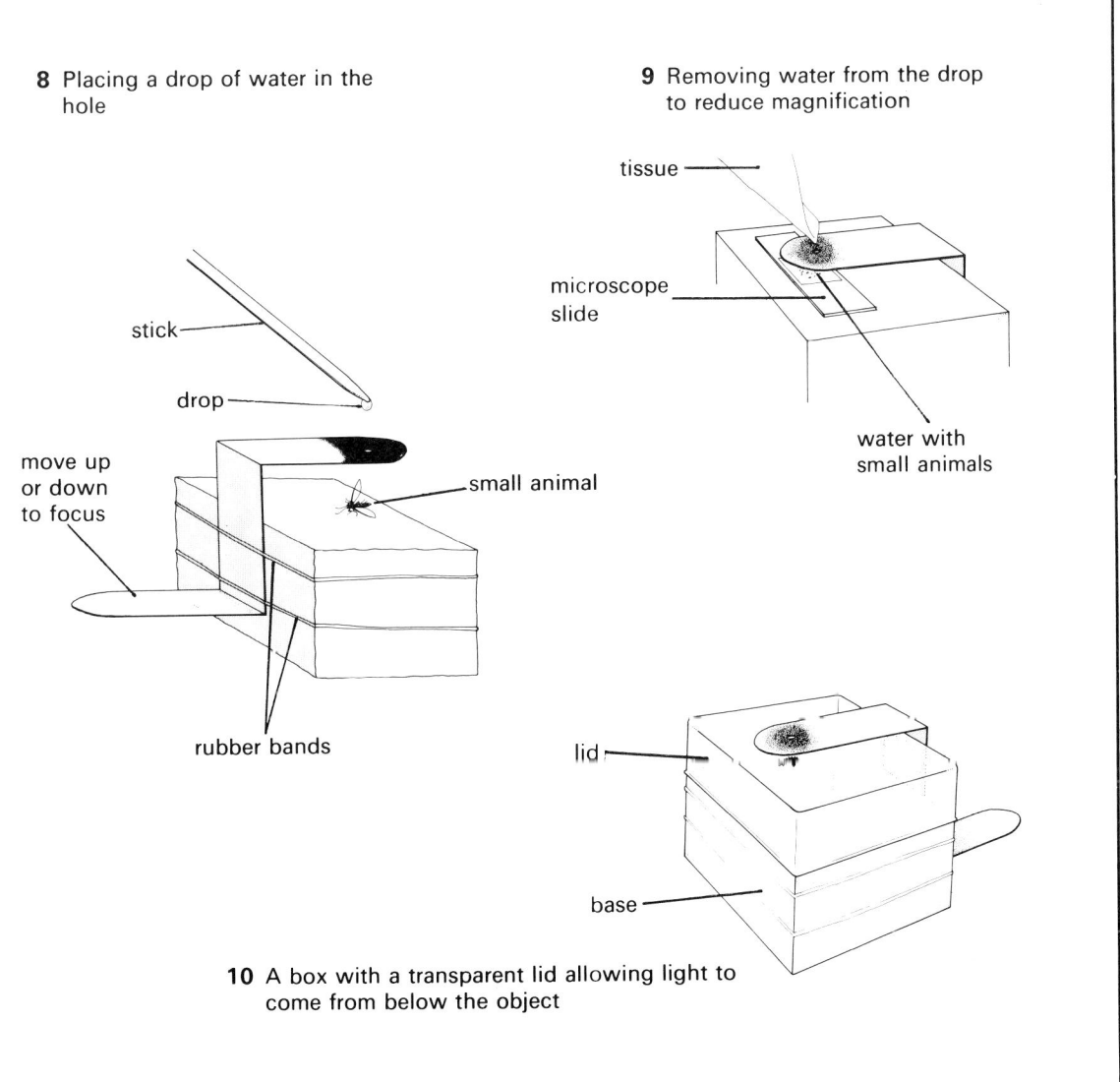

8 Placing a drop of water in the hole

9 Removing water from the drop to reduce magnification

10 A box with a transparent lid allowing light to come from below the object candle and tip it so that a drop of wax falls on to the strip and spreads out *around* the hole. Do not let the wax block the hole. Put a drop on the other side too. Add further drops if necessary. Now leave the strip to cool so that the wax sets.

Mount the strip on the box, as in the drawing, and use a sharpened stick to place a small drop of water in the hole. The microscope is now ready for use.

TRYING IT OUT

The drop of water acts as a lens. Since the drop is small and almost spherical, it forms a lens which focuses on very close objects. The secret of using the microscope is to place the drop *close* to the object you wish to look at and to put your eye *close* above the drop.

Try out the microscope on a piece of newspaper. Put a scrap of newspaper on the block or box and lower the strip until the drop is only a few millimetres above the paper. Place your eye close to the drop and adjust the strip slightly up or down until you can see a highly magnified picture of the letters on the newspaper. If you look at the scale of a ruler it will give you an idea of the amount of magnification. If the drop is almost perfectly spherical it may magnify too much. To reduce the magnification soak up some of the water drop by gently touching a piece of paper tissue or blotting paper against it *for an instant*. This will leave a 'flatter' drop which will magnify less than a spherical drop.

In 5 or 10 minutes, evaporation will have made the drop even flatter, and you will need to raise the strip as the focal length increases. Eventually, you will need to replace the drop with a new one.

Certain kinds of object are better seen if they are lit from below. One way of arranging this is to mount the strip on a box like that shown in the drawing. Photographic slides are often returned from processing in boxes of this type, so this may be one source of supply. Alternatively, look in the food cupboard for a suitable plastic container. To increase the amount of light, line the box with aluminium kitchen foil.

ANIMALS TO LOOK AT

You can find plenty of small animals in an aquarium (Chapter 2) or in soil (Chapter 8) as well as in many places in and around the home and garden. To obtain some really small animals, set up a hay infusion, as described below.

Chop some dried grass into small pieces and put it in a saucepan with water. Bring it to the boil and let it simmer for 5 minutes. This makes a kind of 'grass soup' for the animals to feed on.

Let the soup cool and pour it (with the pieces of grass) into a jar or plastic container. Add a few more pieces of grass that have not been boiled: these will provide spores of small animals to grow in the soup. Alternatively, add 2 or 3 teaspoonfuls of soil, or a few dead leaves.

Put the culture, as it shall now be called, in a warm room. Cover it to stop the water from evaporating and leave it undisturbed for 3 or 4 days. Use a squeeze pipette to take a few drops of water from the surface of the culture, trying to disturb the surface as little as possible.

Sampling the surface of the culture to find small animals

squeeze pipette

chopped leaves 'soup' or infusion

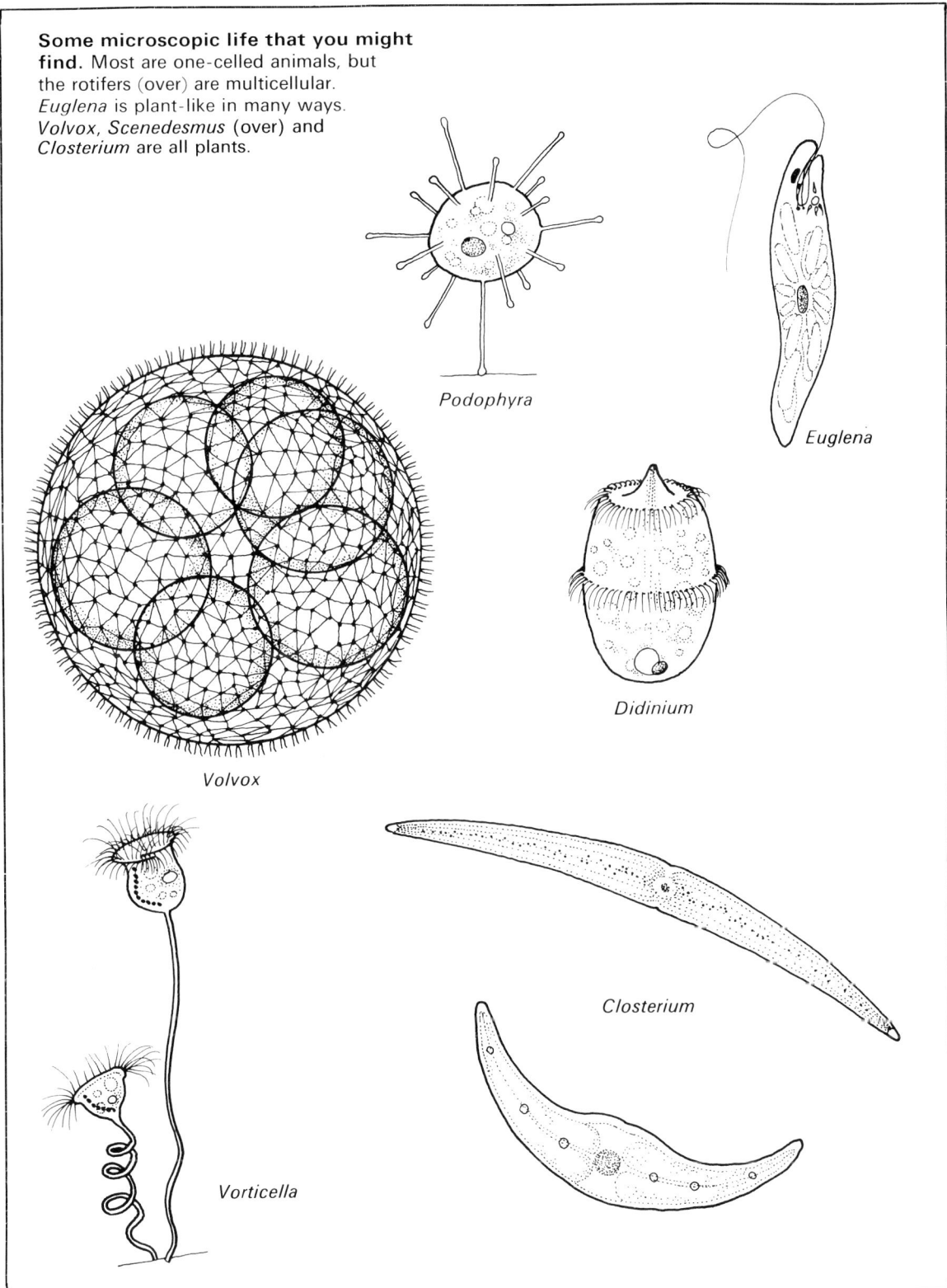

Some microscopic life that you might find. Most are one-celled animals, but the rotifers (over) are multicellular. *Euglena* is plant-like in many ways. *Volvox*, *Scenedesmus* (over) and *Closterium* are all plants.

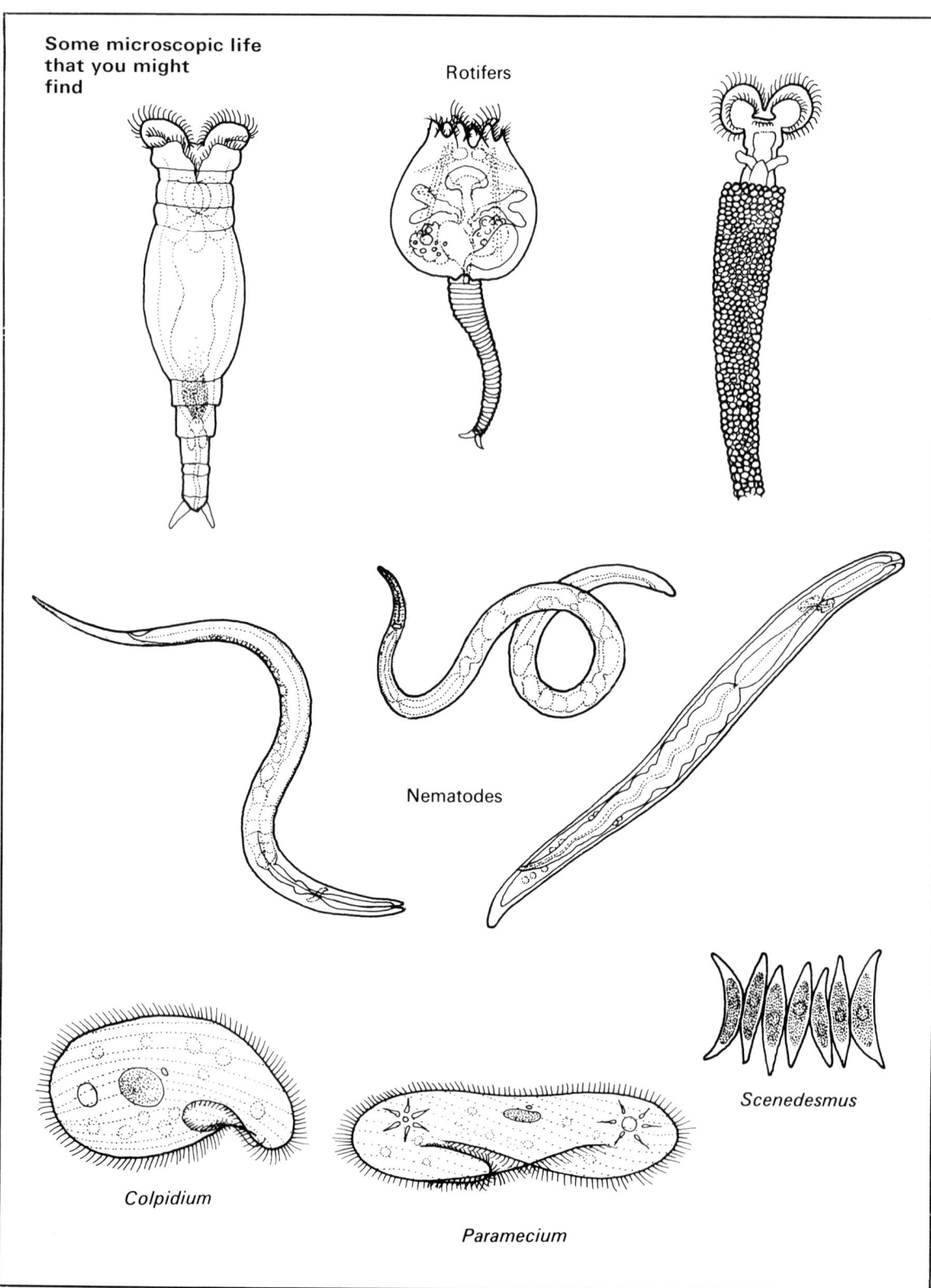

Put the drops on a microscope slide, if you have one, or a strip of stiff transparent plastic, which can be used instead. If your microscope is built from a box with a transparent lid, the drop can be put directly on to the lid. The drawings show some of the animals you are likely to see.

Many of the animals swim so quickly that they do not stay in sight for long. One way to stop them moving so fast is to put a *very small* tuft of cotton-wool in the water. Alternatively, mix some Polycel (or wallpaper adhesive) with water to make a sloppy jelly and then mix a few drops of this with the drops from the culture.

Look at several drops from the surface and near the bottom of the culture. You can also pick out *small* pieces of grass or leaf. Place one of these on the slide and cover with a few drops of water. Look for small animals attached to the leaf or crowding around it for food.

If you examine the culture 2 or 3 days later you will probably find quite a different collection of animals.

6 A wormery

Earthworms are interesting animals to study. Although they are so common and live just beneath the ground, very little is seen of them. You can learn a lot more about worms if you keep them in a wormery.

WHAT YOU NEED

Pieces of timber of the following approximate sizes, (from your local D.I.Y. store):

1 piece 530 mm long by 90 mm wide by 13 mm thick
2 pieces 300 mm long by 70 mm wide by 13 mm thick
1 piece 300 mm long by 32 mm wide by 13 mm thick
2 pieces 284 mm long by 32 mm wide by 13 mm thick
6 pieces of 13 mm quarter-round beading, each 300 mm long

You will also need two pieces of window glass, 300 mm square; two 75 mm iron brackets; some 20 mm panel pins; twelve 10 mm screws for the brackets; a piece of wire or plastic gauze about 300 mm × 75 mm; a sheet of stiff black cardboard; tube of Bostik-1, Evostik (or similar) wood glue; gloss paint.

MAKING THE WORMERY

Use a craft knife to cut *both* ends of two of the pieces of beading, as shown. The gaps between the central strip and the beading must be wide enough for the glass to slip easily into them. The strips and beading are first coated with wood glue on the under surfaces and placed in position. The central strip is more firmly fixed in place by two or three panel pins.

Next, assemble the two sides, as shown, having shaped *one* end of each of the four pieces of beading. Once again, the gaps between the central strip and the beading must be wide enough to hold the glass. When the glue is dry, the sides are then fixed to the base by means of the brackets. Screw the brackets to the sides first. Temporarily, place the glass in position and mark on the base-board the positions of the screw-holes in the brackets. This is to make certain that the frame is wide enough to hold the glass. A loose fit is best so there is less danger of cracking the glass when slipping it in or out. Put the pieces of glass aside while you screw the sides of the frame in position. Afterwards, slide them into their slots to check that they fit properly. Remove the pieces of glass and bore the two drainage holes in the base.

To prevent it from rotting, the frame needs a coat of primer, followed by undercoat and topped by a coat of gloss paint. Rather than buy primer and undercoat specially, you can manage with a coat or two of gloss paint alone. Alternatively, you can varnish the wood or use a spray-can of car paint.

While you are waiting for the paint to dry, make the light-proof cover. This is cut from cardboard and should be matt black on the inside, at least. Make it a loose fit over the frame and deep enough to rest on the base-board.

To make certain that the worms cannot escape, put a piece of wire or plastic gauze over the drainage holes.

GETTING STARTED

You need enough soil to fill the frame. It should not be a heavy clay, but preferably a slightly damp, crumbly garden soil with a little well-rotted compost added to it. Use a small trowel or spade to put the soil into the frame a little at a time. Use a stick to push the soil down evenly, but do not pack it too tightly. If you like, you can put in two or three thin layers of sand. Later, you will be able to see how well the earthworms mix these layers with the rest of the soil. Fill the frame to within 50 mm of the top, then place a few dead leaves on the surface. Put the wormery in a cold room or an outhouse—warm rooms are

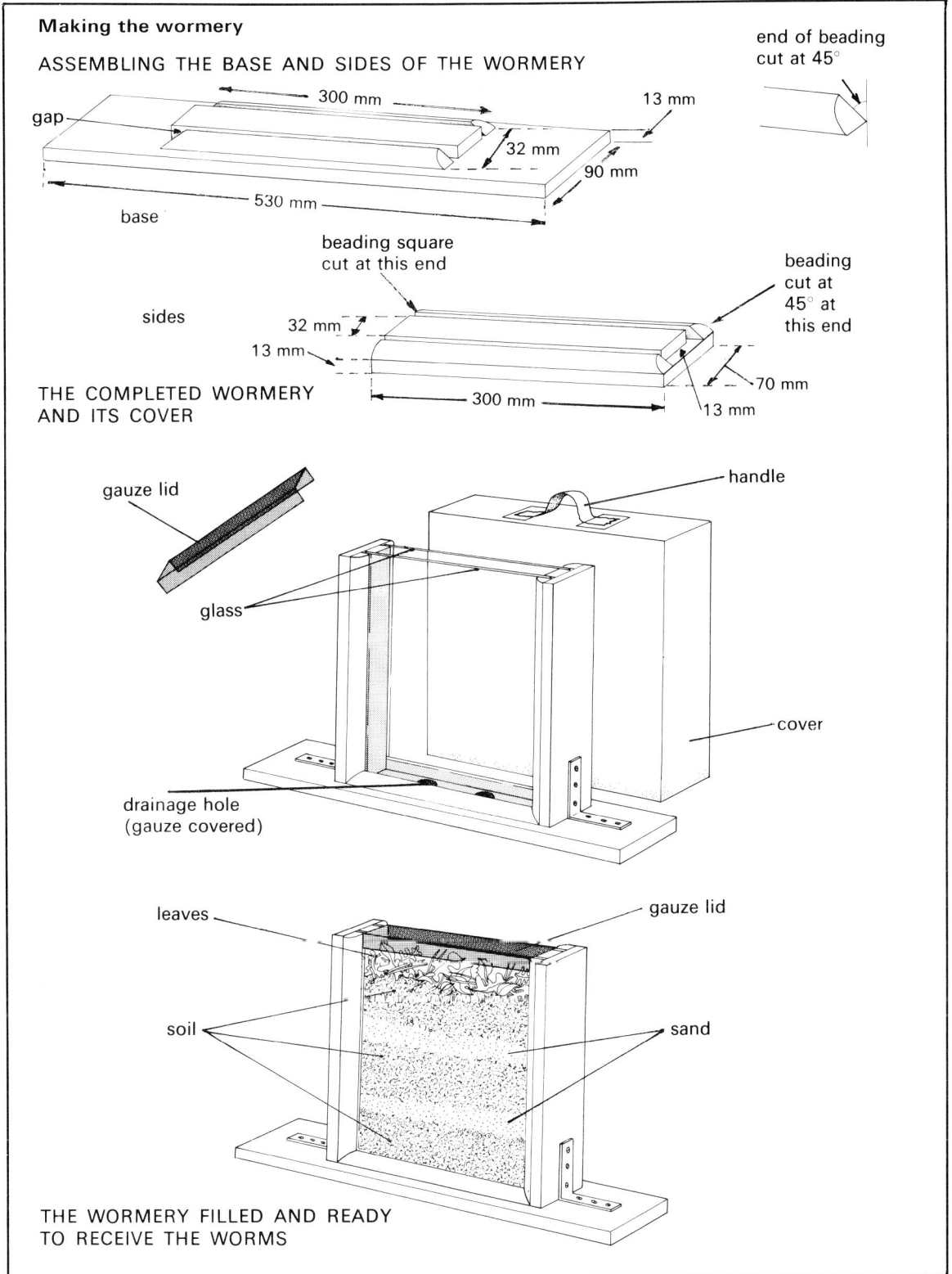

not suitable places in which to keep worms. The soil should be kept moist, but never saturated, by sprinkling it gently with water from time to time.

CATCHING THE WORMS

You need about 5 worms for a wormery of this size. Look for them where fairly large, heavy objects are resting on the soil, for example, under large stones, a garden roller or a log. If the worms start to move into their burrows when disturbed, do not try to pull them back out as they can grip the sides of the burrow very strongly. Have a spade ready to dig up the soil with the worm in it. You will often come across worms when digging a flower-bed or the vegetable patch. Another good place to look is in the soil around or beneath a compost heap. If you go out at night with a torch you will often find worms on the lawn or garden-beds, partly out of their burrows. This is one of the best times for catching worms.

As you catch each worm, put it on top of the soil in the wormery. Put the gauze in position and place the cover over to keep out light. The darkness beneath the cover encourages the worms to tunnel close to the inside of the glass so that you will be able to see them clearly in their burrows. Always replace the cover when you are not actually looking at the worms.

EARTHWORMS AND LONGWORMS

There are many kinds of worm to be found in the garden, each with its own distinctive features and particular habits. The commonest kind is the long earthworm (*Allolobophora*) which produces casts on the surface of the soil. These casts are very noticeable on a lawn. The common earthworm (*Lumbricus*), on the other hand, produces no casts. The drawing shows some other differences.

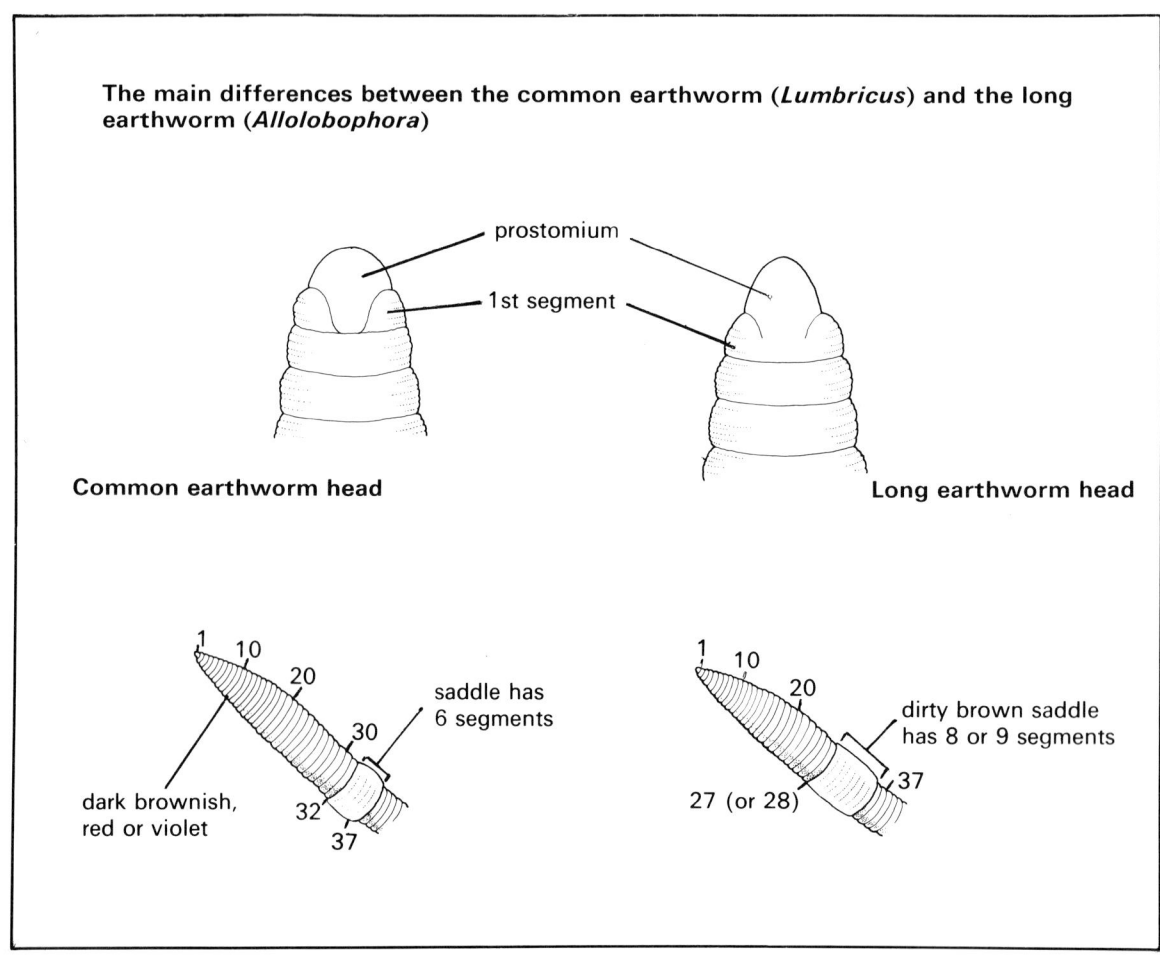

The main differences between the common earthworm (*Lumbricus*) and the long earthworm (*Allolobophora*)

THINGS TO TRY

You can find out lots about your worm by some simple tests. For example, what do they eat? Try putting different kinds of food on the surface and see which they take. Possible foods include leaves from various trees and from other kinds of plant. For a start, try leaves of lime, poplar, sycamore, holly, dandelion and groundsel. Do they prefer fresh leaves or dead leaves? Will they eat stems and roots? Will they eat dead insects or pieces of meat? Do worms feed at *any* time of day or at some particular time? If you can find out *when* they feed you will be able to take off the cover at that time and watch them feeding.

Watch them as they move and try to work out what happens. How do they grip the soil? Try running your finger along the side of the worm and you will find this out. Or let the worms crawl on dry newspaper and listen to them carefully.

Some kinds of worm plug their burrows by pulling leaves down into the opening. Do they prefer certain kinds of leaf for this? Do they also eat the leaves they use for plugging?

You may be lucky enough to find two of the worms mating. This is most likely to occur at night. Try to extract the egg capsule from the wormery and keep it as described below. As you should change the soil in the wormery every few weeks, this is the time to search through the soil for egg capsules. They are hard, coloured brown and about 5 mm long. If you find any, put them in a small box or jar to hatch out. Line the container with damp moss to keep the atmosphere moist. Although each cocoon contains several eggs, usually only one egg hatches to become a worm.

7 Keeping caterpillars

The caterpillars (or larvae) of moths and butterflies go through several stages of growth and shed their skins between each stage. When the larvae are fully grown they become chrysalids (or pupae). There is plenty to watch when you keep caterpillars: the caterpillar becoming a chrysalis, the adult (or imago) butterfly or moth emerging from the chrysalis, the adult butterfly unfolding and drying its wings. You can also watch it feed before letting it free.

WHAT YOU NEED

One or more cages for the caterpillars—you can buy these (see address on p. 60), or use the spider cage (Chapter 1) or make your own special caterpillar cage. To make your own cage, you need one or two *large* plastic bottles (such as those in which squash or cooking oil is sold, the 4 litre size); a piece of nylon netting about 10 cm square; a large rubber band; acetate sheet (not essential); sticky tape (such as Sellotape); cotton-wool; a small jam jar or a pickle jar (no lids). For handling the small caterpillars, you need a medium-sized water-colour paint-brush.

GETTING STARTED

If you do not already have a suitable cage, make one or more as shown in the drawings. Type A is the easiest to make and costs least, though it is harder to see the caterpillars in this kind of cage. If the container held cooking oil, scrub it out well with detergent, then rinse it in clean water and dry it. Type B is an improved version of Type A with an acetate window (or you could use netting or a sheet of clear plastic). Type C is more like the larval cages you can buy. Place the cage where it will not be disturbed and where direct sunlight cannot fall on it.

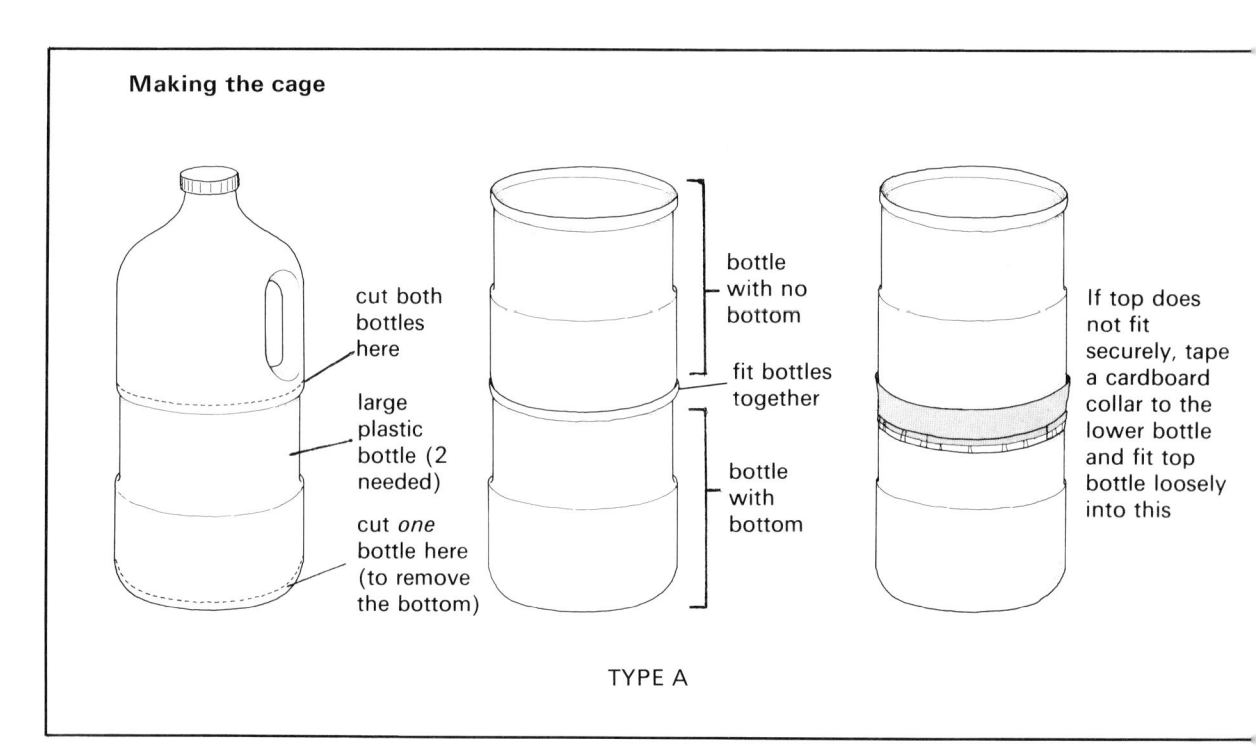

Making the cage

TYPE A

STOCKING THE CAGE

There are three ways of stocking the cage:

1 *Collecting eggs.* This is the most interesting way as you can then follow through the complete life-cycle of the butterfly. Butterfly eggs may be laid on a wide variety of plants, though each type of butterfly has its preferences. Most butterfly books, for example *The Observer's Book of Butterflies* by W. J. Stokoe (Warne), list the plants on which eggs are laid. Several butterflies, including the Small Tortoise-shell, Peacock and Red Admiral, lay their eggs on stinging nettles. A nettle patch is a good place to watch for egg-laying, especially during May and June. The white butterflies lay their eggs on plants of the cabbage family and also on the garden nasturtium in May to August. Look for a butterfly laying its eggs. Butterflies spend a lot of their time sucking nectar from flowers, but occasionally you will see one settle for a short while on a leaf or stem, then fly away. Look at the spot where the butterfly settled, usually on the *lower* side of the leaf. A hand-lens is useful to help you find the eggs. Collect the leaves and stems of the plant that the eggs have been laid on, and put them in the cage in a pot of water together with a few more leaves

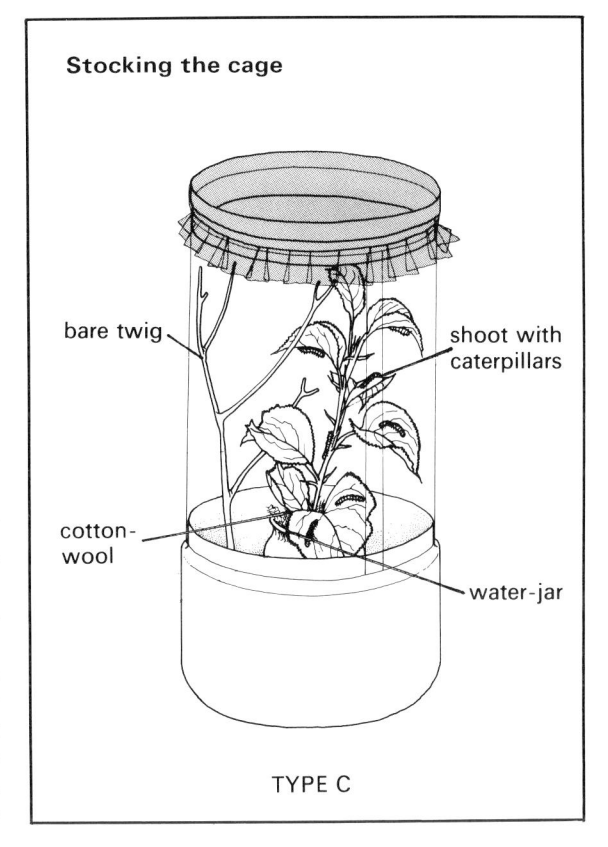

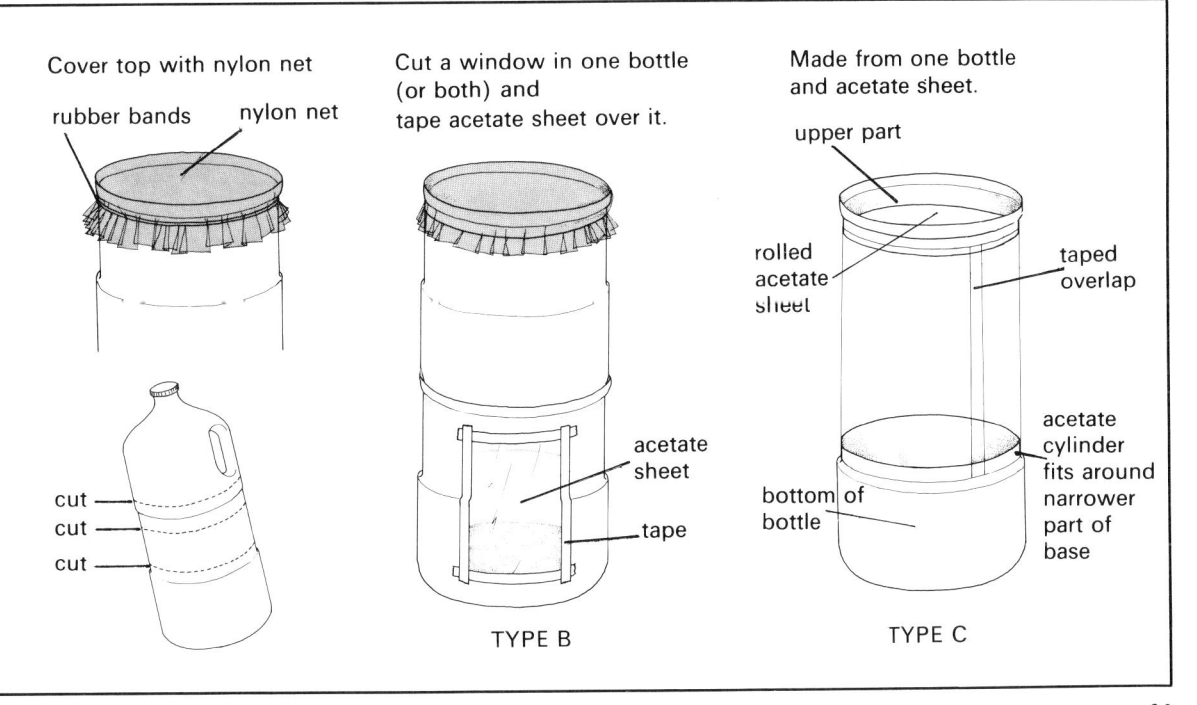

Stocking the cage

TYPE C

Cover top with nylon net
- rubber bands
- nylon net
- cut
- cut
- cut

Cut a window in one bottle (or both) and tape acetate sheet over it.
- acetate sheet
- tape

TYPE B

Made from one bottle and acetate sheet.
- upper part
- rolled acetate sheet
- taped overlap
- bottom of bottle
- acetate cylinder fits around narrower part of base

TYPE C

Some butterfly caterpillars and their eggs

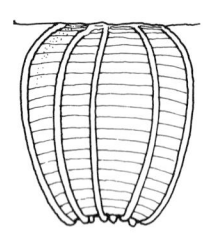

Peacock egg

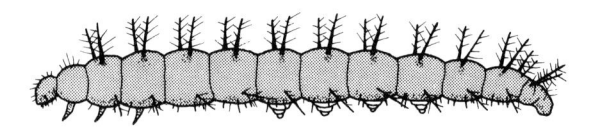

Peacock

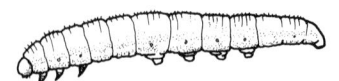

Small White

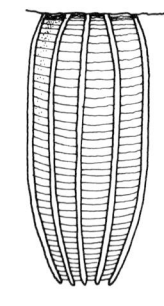

Small White egg

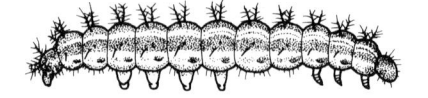

Small Tortoiseshell

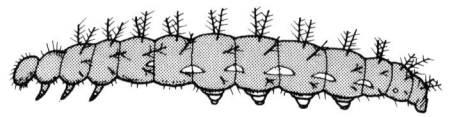

Red Admiral

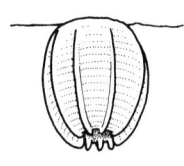

Small Tortoiseshell egg

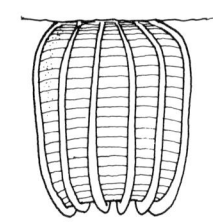

Red Admiral egg

(*The eggs are all 1–2 mm long*)

Two moth caterpillars

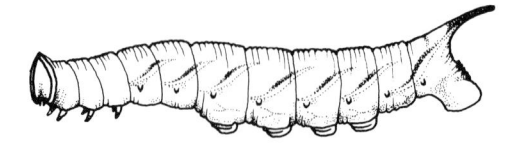

Lime Hawk

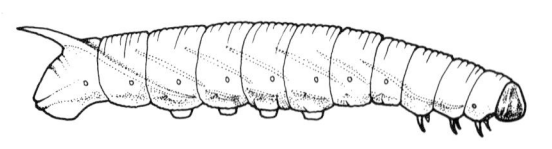

Poplar Hawk

1 cm

or shoots of the same kind. Remember to plug the top of the water-jar securely with cotton-wool so there is no chance of any of the hatching caterpillars falling into the water. Make sure that the cotton-wool does not dip into the water and become saturated. In general, conditions in the cage should not be damp. If condensation collects on the inside of the cage, wipe it off with a cloth or tissue. Do not cram the cage with leaves, for this often leads to condensation and makes it harder to see the caterpillars. As soon as the eggs hatch you will need to provide a plentiful supply of the plant that the caterpillar feeds on. Always provide the same kind of plant as that on which the eggs were laid.

2 *Collecting caterpillars.* Search stinging nettles, plants of the cabbage family and garden nasturtiums from May to August. Also look for hawk-moth caterpillars on apple, poplar and lime trees. The caterpillars are most often found on the lower side of the leaves, which usually show signs of being eaten away at the edges. Collect the leaves with caterpillars on them and also some more leaves or shoots of the same kind. Put the leaves in the pot of water in the cage, taking care to plug the pot with cotton-wool, as described above. To avoid dampness, do not put too many leaves in the cage.

3 *Buying eggs or caterpillars from dealers.* The farms listed on p. 60 supply eggs and larvae of a few common species in season. It is best to write for a list or catalogue so that you can place your order in good time.

LOOKING AFTER THE CATERPILLARS

The most important thing when keeping caterpillars is to give them plenty of fresh food. Replace wilting or mostly-eaten leaves with fresh leaves of the same kind. When the caterpillars are small they can be transferred from the old leaves to the new ones with a paint-brush. To pick them up, moisten the paint-brush slightly, draw out the bristles to make a fine point, and pick up a larva with the tip of the brush and put it gently on to the new plant. It is best to avoid handling the larvae at any later stage. If you have two jars, one jar filled with new leaves, it may be placed beside the old one so that the bunches of leaves are touching. The caterpillars will soon crawl across on to the new leaves.

Caterpillars produce fairly large quantities of droppings which collect at the bottom of the cage. If left, these tend to go mouldy, so tip them out each day. Many kinds of caterpillar need to move to a firm support to moult their skin—the twigs in the cage serve this purpose. Do not disturb a caterpillar while it is moulting or it will not be able to complete the process properly and may die.

CHRYSALIDS

After a few weeks (or maybe only a week or two, if you began with well-developed caterpillars) the caterpillars will be fully grown and ready to become chrysalids. Some, such as the caterpillars of the white butterfly, fix their chrysalids to a vertical surface, e.g. a twig or the wall of the cage. Others, such as the caterpillars of the hawk-moth, bury themselves in soil before turning into chrysalids. If you are rearing those kinds that burrow into the soil, put some soil in the bottom of the cage when you see that they are fully grown. If you see the caterpillars crawling around on the bottom of the cage, you will know it is time to put some soil there. Use bulb-fibre, peat or a loose soil mixed with compost.

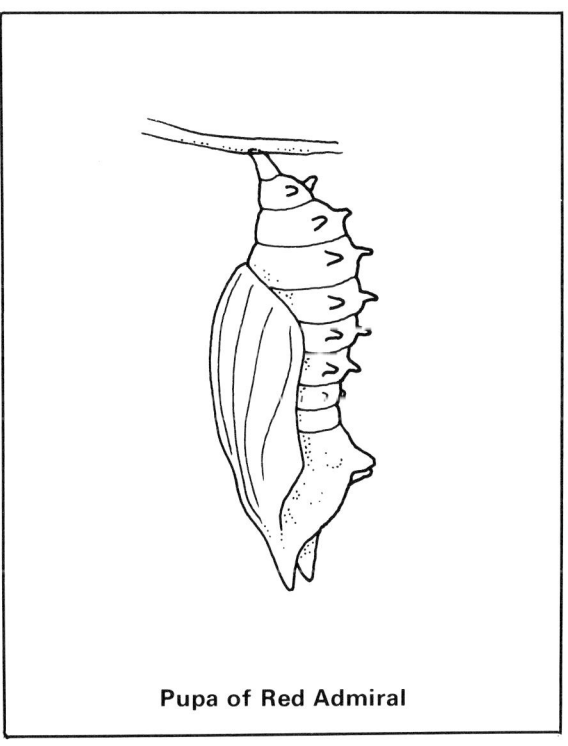

Pupa of Red Admiral

Red Admiral

Peacock

Chrysalids taken from soil can be handled as soon as they have hardened. If it is late in the year (September onwards), they will probably not hatch until next spring (April). You can keep them in a small plastic box until then.

When hatching is due, put them back in the cage on *slightly* damp soil. A little moss on the surface will help keep them damp, but not too damp. Chrysalids that are attached to twigs or the walls of the cage should be left where they are.

When the butterfly or moth hatches, it will need something to climb on to while it spreads and dries its wings. Put a few bare twigs in the cage ready for this. Do not disturb the adult at this stage.

ADULTS

If you would like to see the adult butterfly feeding, put some leafy shoots in the cage, with a few drops of honey on the leaves. Use the runny kind of honey or mix some water with the stiffer kind to make it runny. When you have become really used to handling butterflies you could try to breed from them. A useful guide to this is *Studying Insects* by R. L. E. Ford (Warne). To begin with it is best to keep the adults for no more than a day, then let them free.

8 Life in leaves and soil

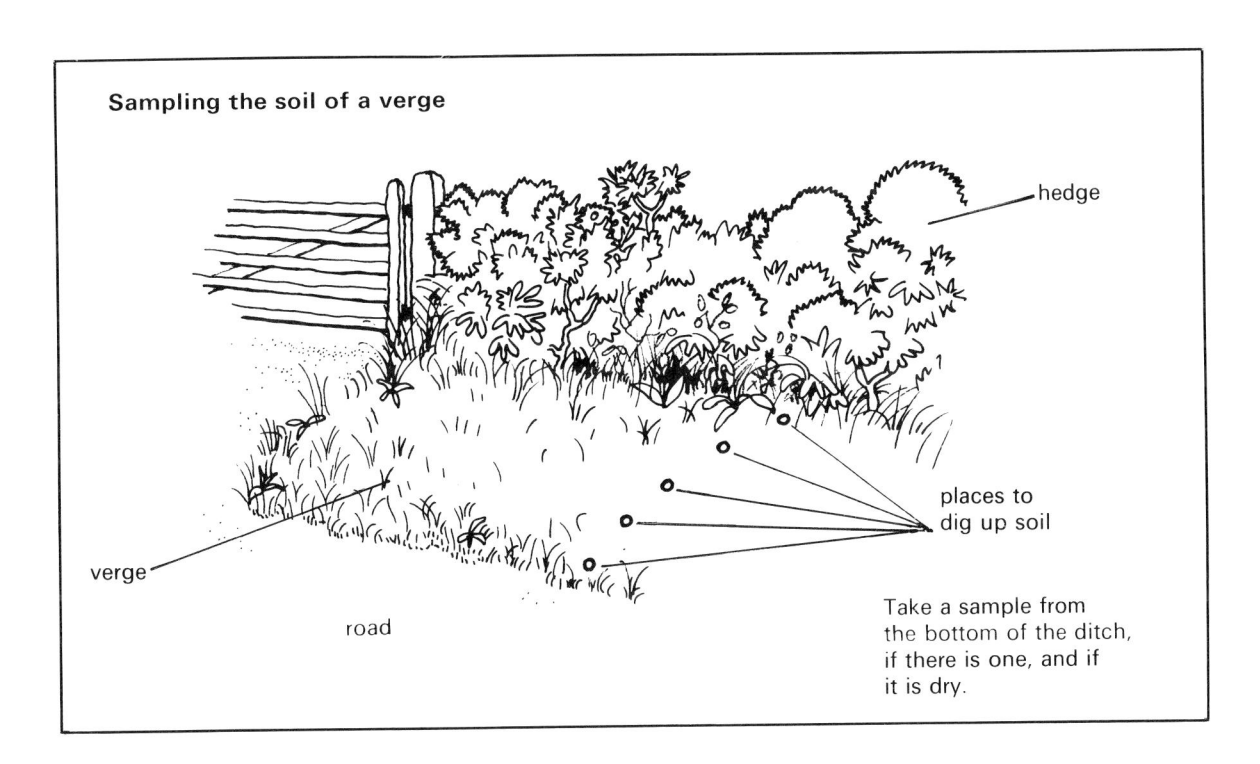

Sampling the soil of a verge

hedge

places to dig up soil

verge

road

Take a sample from the bottom of the ditch, if there is one, and if it is dry.

It is surprising how many different kinds of small animals live in the soil. Many more kinds still, live in the layers of dead leaves found on the soil in woods or under hedges, but their colouring makes them hard to see. Often they stay quite still when disturbed and for some time afterwards, making it even more difficult to spot them. The funnel described in this chapter makes the animals come out of the soil or leaves so that you can see what they look like and find out how many there are.

WHAT YOU NEED

A wire or plastic sieve. Ideally the meshes should be 2 mm apart but if your sieve is slightly finer than this it will not matter. It is best if the sieve is flat-bottomed, but you can use a round-bottomed kitchen sieve if this is what you can get most easily.

Other items needed are: some plastic sandwich bags (with wire-ties); a roll of brown or black paper, smooth and glossy on one side at least; a desk-lamp with a 25 watt bulb; sticky tape (Sellotape); a small jar; materials for making the support for the funnel (see over); some paper tissues; a trowel; a medium-sized water-colour paint-brush; a hand-lens.

MAKING THE FUNNEL

The unit consists of the following four sections, from the top downward:

1 A lamp (25 watt) to dry the soil slowly. As the top layers become dried out the animals move downward. Finally, as the soil dries out completely, they leave the bottom layer of soil.

2 A sieve or grid to support the soil. The holes must be big enough to let the animals pass through them.

Making the funnel

SECTION THROUGH THE FUNNEL TO SHOW THE MAIN PARTS

Labels: shade, low power lamp, gap, sieve, soil sample, gap, funnel (black or brown paper), smooth surface, collecting jar, damp paper tissue, the catch

A FUNNEL MADE FROM A KITCHEN SIEVE

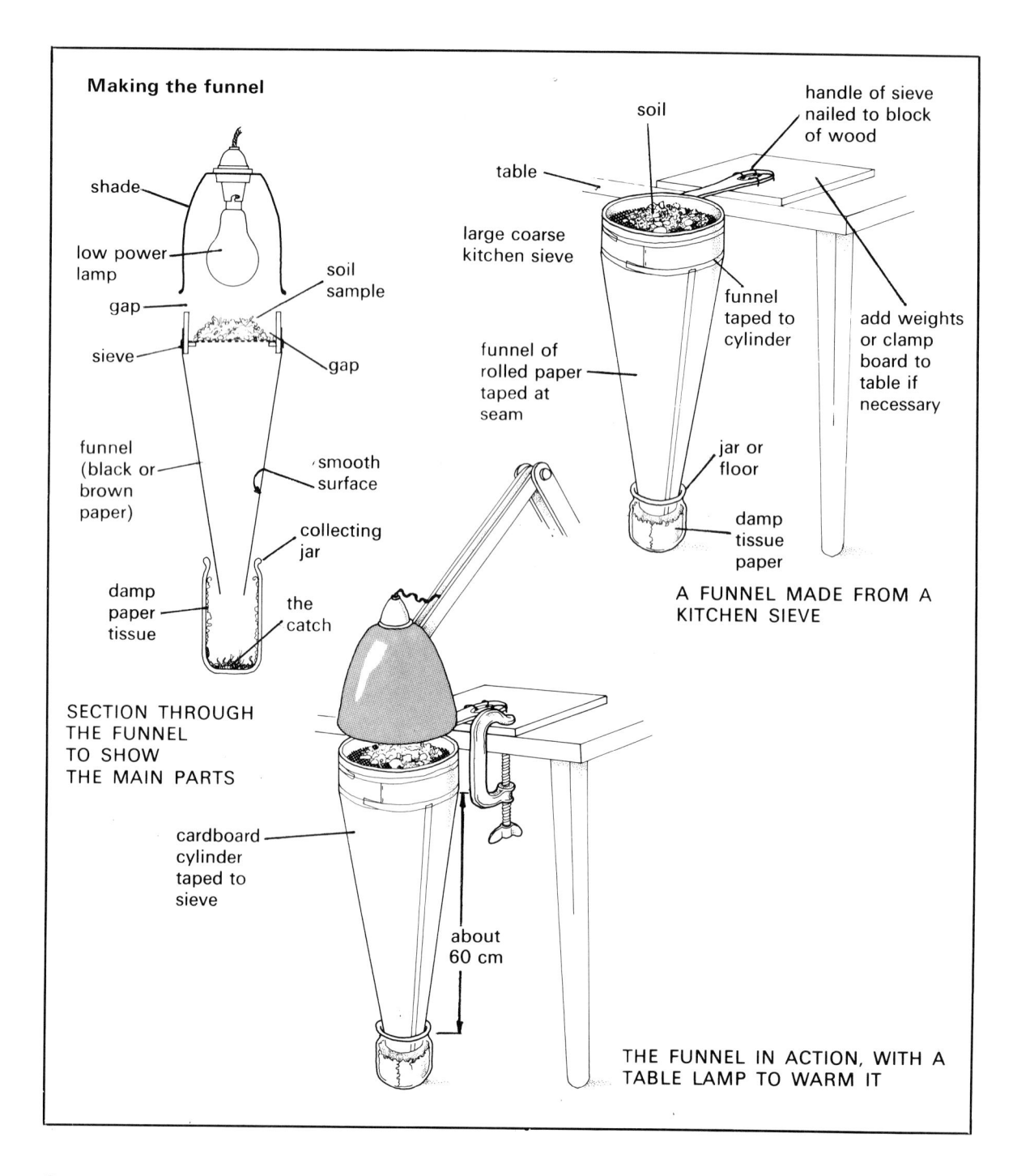

Labels: soil, handle of sieve nailed to block of wood, table, large coarse kitchen sieve, funnel taped to cylinder, add weights or clamp board to table if necessary, funnel of rolled paper taped at seam, jar or floor, damp tissue paper

THE FUNNEL IN ACTION, WITH A TABLE LAMP TO WARM IT

Labels: cardboard cylinder taped to sieve, about 60 cm

3 A long funnel with a slippery surface inside so that the animals fall down the funnel.

4 A jar to collect the animals as they fall out of the funnel. The jar should be lined with damp paper tissue to keep the animals alive.

Exactly how you make your funnel depends on what kind of lamp, sieve and other items you have been able to collect. It does not matter if you do not have exactly the same things as are shown in the drawing; alter the design to suit what you have.

38

GETTING STARTED

Dig up a trowelful of soil from a garden-bed, put it in a plastic bag, and seal the bag with a 'wire-tie'. The soil can be kept in the bag for a day or two if you do not want to use it straight away. To be sure of finding plenty of animals it is best to collect rich, loose, moist soil from a well-cultivated garden-bed, or from a hedge-bank. Avoid areas that have been sprayed with insecticides.

Take away the collecting bottle while you put the soil on the sieve. Pile the soil on to the sieve, about 3 cm deep, leaving a gap of at least 1 cm around the edges of the soil to allow air to circulate and dry the soil. Now tap the funnel to dislodge any pieces of soil that have fallen into it. Moisten the tissue in the jar and put the jar under the funnel.

At first you may need several trials to get the right amount of heating from the bulb. If the heat is too gentle, it will take days to dry the soil. If it is too strong, the soil will be dry before the animals have had a chance to move out of it and they will die in the soil. Begin with a 25 watt bulb placed about 5 cm above the soil. If you have a thermometer, measure the temperature of the soil after about 2 hours. If it is more than 30 °C, move the bulb further from the soil. If it is much less, try using a 40 watt bulb instead. The lamp must be left on day and night until no more animals appear in the jar. This may take up to 2 or 3 days, depending on the type of soil and how damp it was to start with. Do not wait all this time before examining your catch. Look at the jar several times each day. It is a good idea to remove the complete catch on each occasion, using the brush, as described on p. 35. You can find out what group an animal belongs to by using the chart on p. 40–41. Then you can either put it back on to the soil it came from or, before doing this, keep it for a day or two in a small container lined with damp paper tissue. It is important to remove carnivorous animals such as centipedes as soon as you see them, otherwise they will rapidly eat the remainder of your catch.

MORE THINGS TO TRY

Compare the populations of soils of different kinds or from different depths. Collect the animals from the soils on the same day using separate funnels at the same time, one for each soil. If you have only one funnel, test the other soils as soon as possible after the first is finished.

The funnel can also be used for extracting small animals from leaf litter. This is the layer of dead and decaying leaves that you find beneath trees

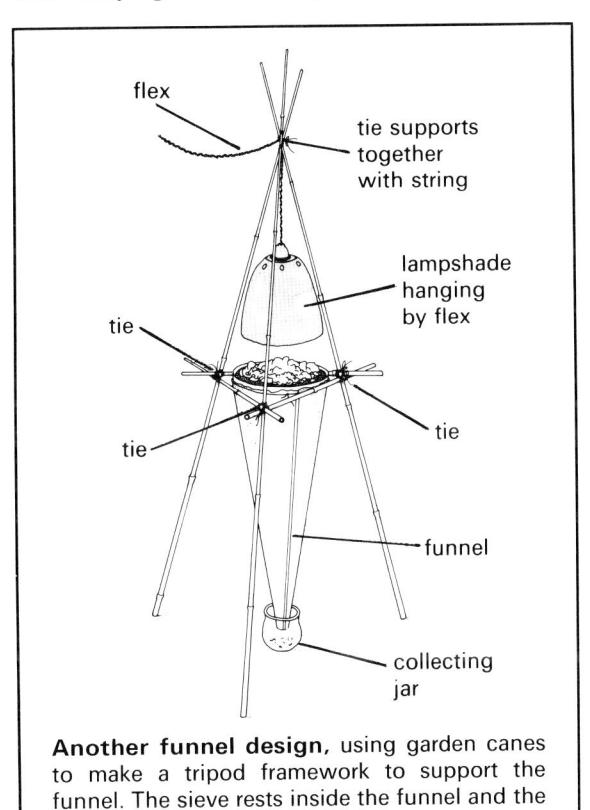

Another funnel design, using garden canes to make a tripod framework to support the funnel. The sieve rests inside the funnel and the handle (if any) may be cut off

and hedges. The litter is a food for many kinds of small animal, so you would expect to find lots of animals in it. Another similar material is the partly rotted plant material in garden compost heaps. In all of these places you will find a wide variety of interesting small animals.

LARGER SOIL ANIMALS

To look for soil animals which are too large to pass through the sieve make a salt solution by dissolving 9 tablespoonfuls of cooking salt in 1½ litres (2½ pints) of water. Pour on enough salt solution to cover a trowelful of soil, spread out in a shallow glass or plastic dish, and stir slightly. Pick off the animals which float to the surface with a paint-brush or a small spoon, and rinse them in clean water before examining them.

A FLOW CHART TO HELP YOU IDENTIFY

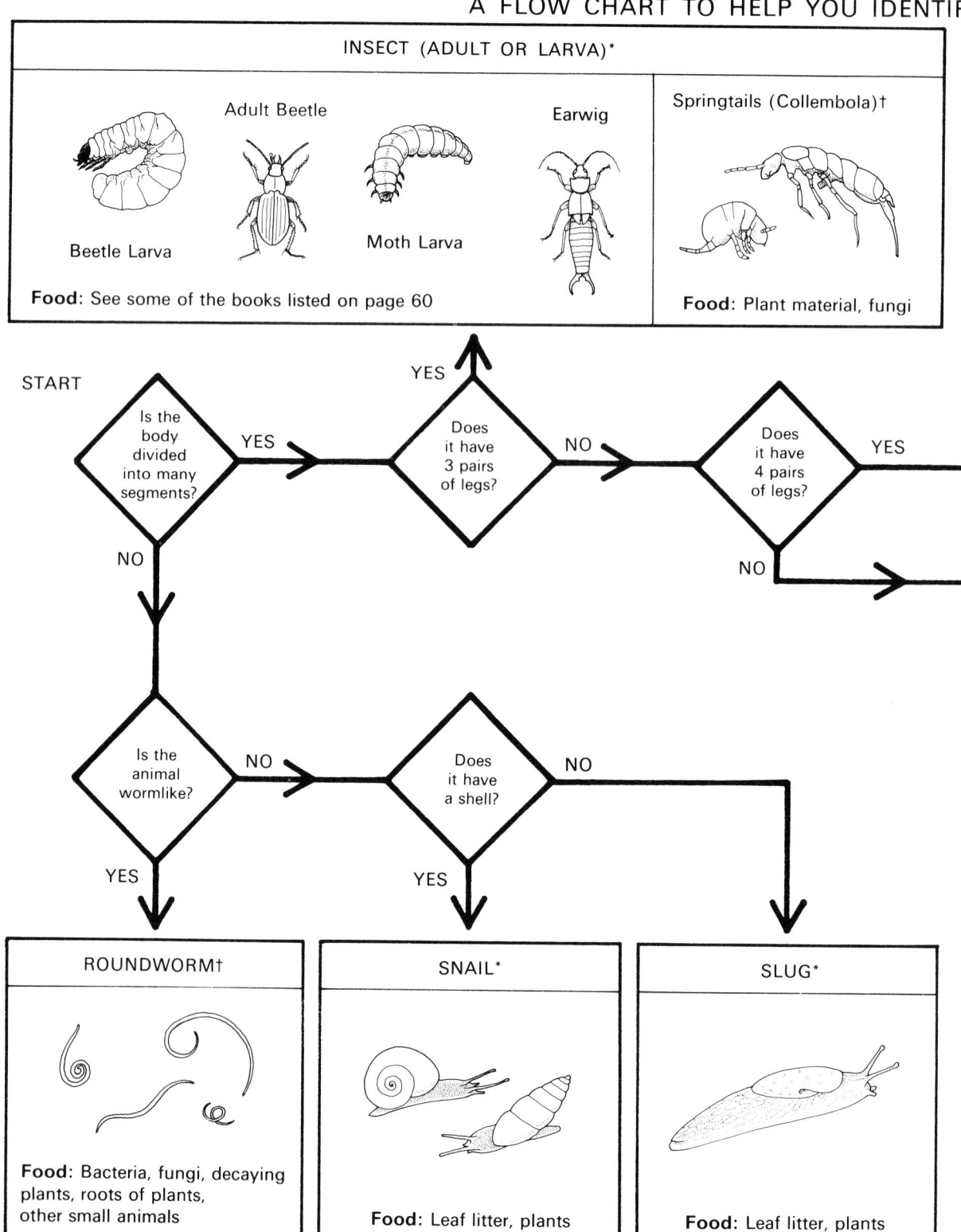

INSECT (ADULT OR LARVA)*

- Beetle Larva
- Adult Beetle
- Moth Larva
- Earwig
- Springtails (Collembola)†

Food: See some of the books listed on page 60

Food: Plant material, fungi

START

- Is the body divided into many segments?
  - YES → Does it have 3 pairs of legs?
    - YES → (Insect)
    - NO → Does it have 4 pairs of legs?
      - YES →
      - NO →
  - NO → Is the animal wormlike?
    - YES → ROUNDWORM†
    - NO → Does it have a shell?
      - YES → SNAIL*
      - NO → SLUG*

ROUNDWORM†

Food: Bacteria, fungi, decaying plants, roots of plants, other small animals

SNAIL*

Food: Leaf litter, plants

SLUG*

Food: Leaf litter, plants

*Larger ones are often too big for the funnel   †Very common in most soils

ANIMALS FROM SOIL AND LEAF LITTER

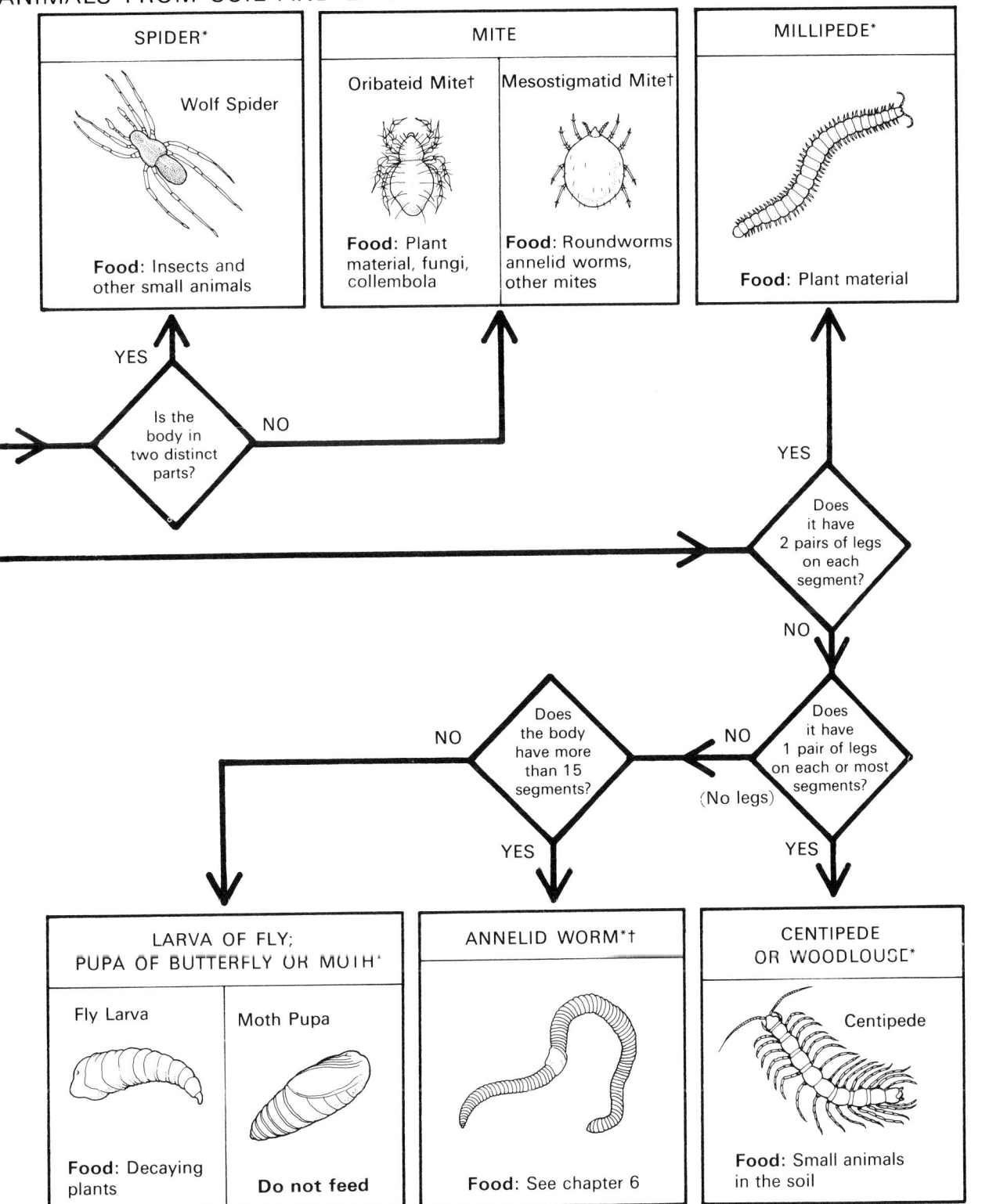

SPIDER*
Wolf Spider

Food: Insects and other small animals

MITE

Oribateid Mite†

Food: Plant material, fungi, collembola

Mesostigmatid Mite†

Food: Roundworms annelid worms, other mites

MILLIPEDE*

Food: Plant material

Is the body in two distinct parts?
- YES → SPIDER
- NO → MITE

Does it have 2 pairs of legs on each segment?
- YES → MILLIPEDE
- NO ↓

Does it have 1 pair of legs on each or most segments?
- YES → CENTIPEDE OR WOODLOUSE
- NO (No legs) ↓

Does the body have more than 15 segments?
- NO → LARVA OF FLY; PUPA OF BUTTERFLY OR MOTH
- YES → ANNELID WORM

LARVA OF FLY; PUPA OF BUTTERFLY OR MOTH*

Fly Larva

Food: Decaying plants

Moth Pupa

Do not feed

ANNELID WORM*†

Food: See chapter 6

CENTIPEDE OR WOODLOUSE*

Centipede

Food: Small animals in the soil

41

9 Making a microhabitat

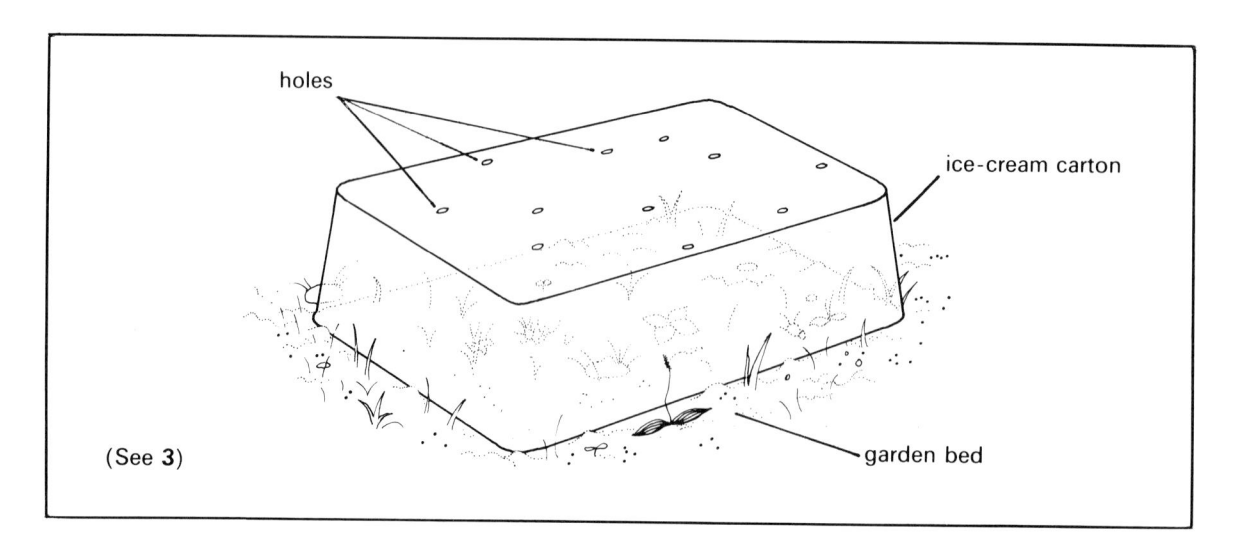

Diagram showing an ice-cream carton with holes placed upside down on a garden bed. (See 3)

A *habitat* is a place where animals and plants can live, e.g. a lake, a cliff, a meadow or a wood. Microhabitats are habitats on a small scale, e.g. a pile of dead leaves, a hollow tree, a puddle or a stone wall. Many animals, usually *small* animals, live all or most of their lives in one microhabitat. There they find all they need—food and water, protection from too much heat or too much cold, space to live in, a place to hide away from animals which might eat them, and a good chance of meeting other animals of the same kind as themselves so that they can reproduce.

You can find dozens of natural microhabitats simply by looking out for them, or you can make your own.

WHAT YOU NEED

To decide what you need, first think about what the small animals need. They need *food*, *shelter*, a *space* to live and they need to be *protected*. Of course, you cannot hope to provide them with *everything* they need, but you must try to provide something to encourage them to come to your microhabitat. The suggestions below will help you decide what you (and the animals) need.

GETTING STARTED

Try one or more of these ideas:

1 Leave a pile of old sacks on the soil in some damp, shady corner of the garden. You can also use an old coconut-fibre doormat or pieces of fibreboard.

2 Make a hay infusion (Chapter 5) and leave it uncovered on a shady window-sill for several weeks, topping it up with cooled, boiled water when necessary.

3 Put a large transparent plastic container (e.g. a used ice-cream carton) upside down on a corner of a garden-bed or lawn. If you make a few small holes in the container, it will help to ventilate it and allow small animals to get in. Water the soil and the container from time to time.

4 Make a pile of leaf litter on the soil in a damp, shady corner of the garden.

5 Take some damp leaf litter and seal it in a plastic container (the ice-cream carton).

6 Buy or make a nesting box. Birds may use it for rearing their young, or other small animals may come to live on it.

about half full
sealed with lid
ice-cream carton
leaf litter

(See **5**)

9. Place a flowerpot upside down on the soil.
10. Bury a flowerpot so the top is level with the soil surface and fill it with soil. Water it often to keep the soil really damp. (See over.)
11. Make a mini-aquarium and leave it on the window-sill.
12. When you are in the country look for a rotting log or branch—even in the town, it is often possible to find a piece of rotting timber. Half bury the log or timber in soil in a part of the garden where it will stay damp, or put it on a shaded window-sill in a plastic container (ice-cream carton). Punch a few holes in the container to allow a *little* ventilation. (See over.)

These ideas may lead you to think of some even better ideas of your own.

WHAT TO DO NEXT

Look at the habitat once or twice a week for several weeks. There may be nothing much to see at first, but you will usually be rewarded in the end. If no animals appear, check that the conditions in the habitat are suitable. Is it too hot? too cold? too dry? too wet? Is there any food? You could try various foods: seeds (wild bird seed), rotting leaves or compost, sugar syrup (or molasses), or dead insects. Some animals feed on living plants; even if no animals come at first they

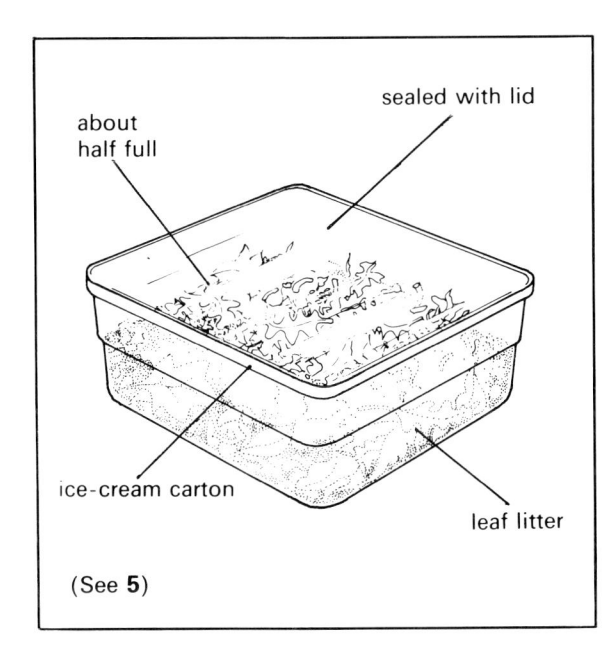

7. Make a pile of stones on the soil in a damp shady corner of the garden, putting the biggest stones at the bottom. Animals will come to live among the stones *and* in the soil beneath the stones.
8. Get some air-bricks and put them in long grass or under bushes. Look for animals living in the tubes.

bushes
air-bricks
undergrowth

(See **8**)

(See **10**)

water often

rotting log

holes

soil

ice-cream carton

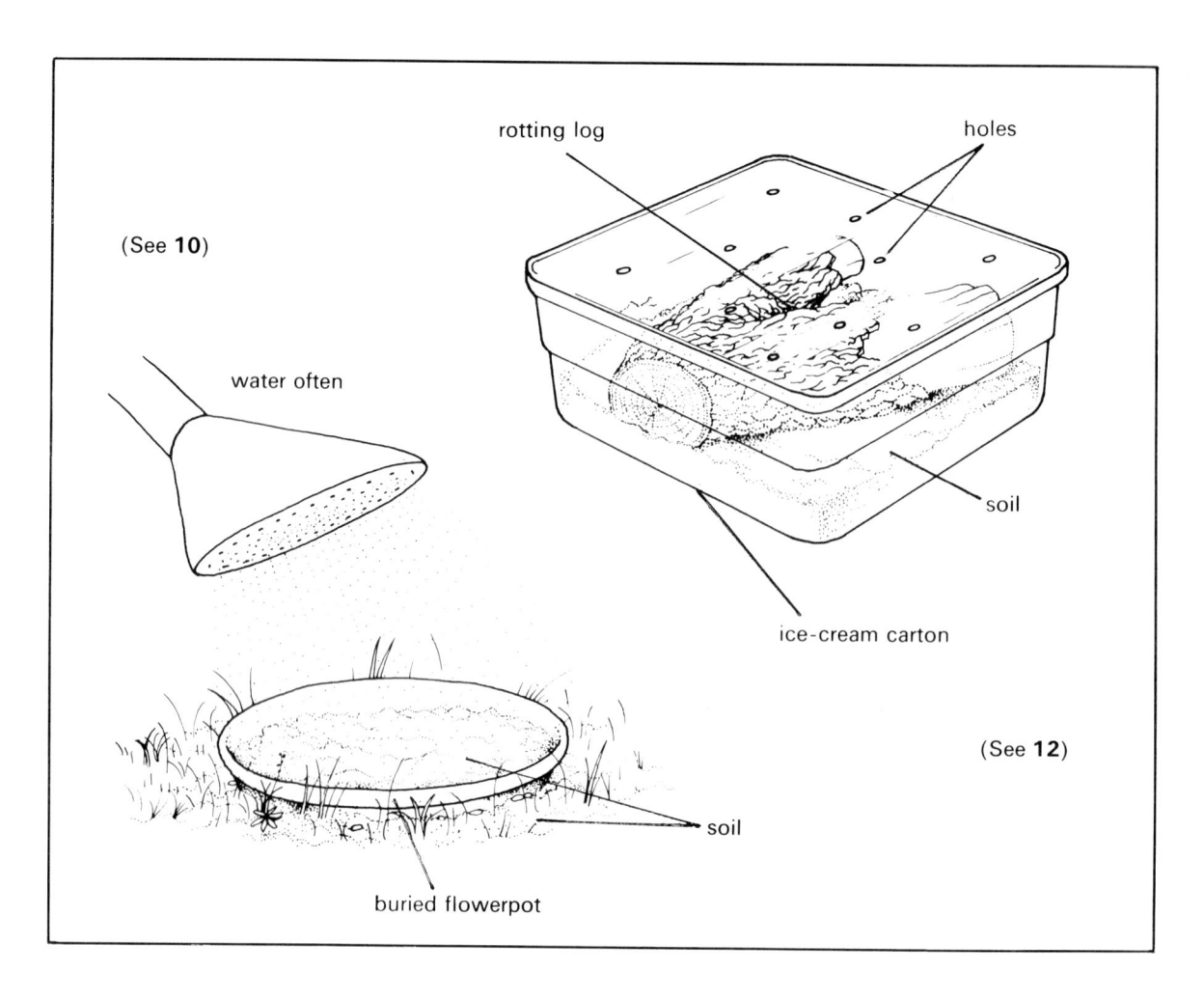

(See **12**)

buried flowerpot

soil

may come later if plants begin to grow in the microhabitat. The word 'plants' includes mosses and algae which may grow after a while in damp habitats (e.g. **2**, **10** and **12**).

The animals may be there but it may not be easy to see them because they are too small; therefore use the microscope (Chapter 5). Alternatively, use the funnel described in Chapter 8 to find the animals in leaf litter soil or rotting timber.

GETTING THERE

Animals cannot appear from nowhere. Somehow they have to get to your microhabitat. If your microhabitat is on a window-sill that is twenty floors up a high-rise block, the animals will need to fly to reach it. If you live in the centre of a large town, they may need to fly a long way. Your microhabitat may be without occupants for a long time, but usually some animals will reach it in the end. One way over this problem is to bring the animals to the habitat. Some materials have the animals in them to begin with. Leaf litter, soil and rotting timber contain small animals. They may also contain the eggs, spores or pupae of other small animals that will hatch out when you have put the material in your microhabitat. So, particularly if you live in a large town and have no garden, bring animals to the microhabitat by putting materials of these kinds in it.

WHAT TO DO NEXT

A microhabitat can last for months or years. Keep a note of all the animals you find in it. Try to work out why they are there. Are they there to get food? Are they there for shelter? You may find that the animals which first come to the microhabitat are eaten by animals which arrive later.

10 The world of the woodlouse

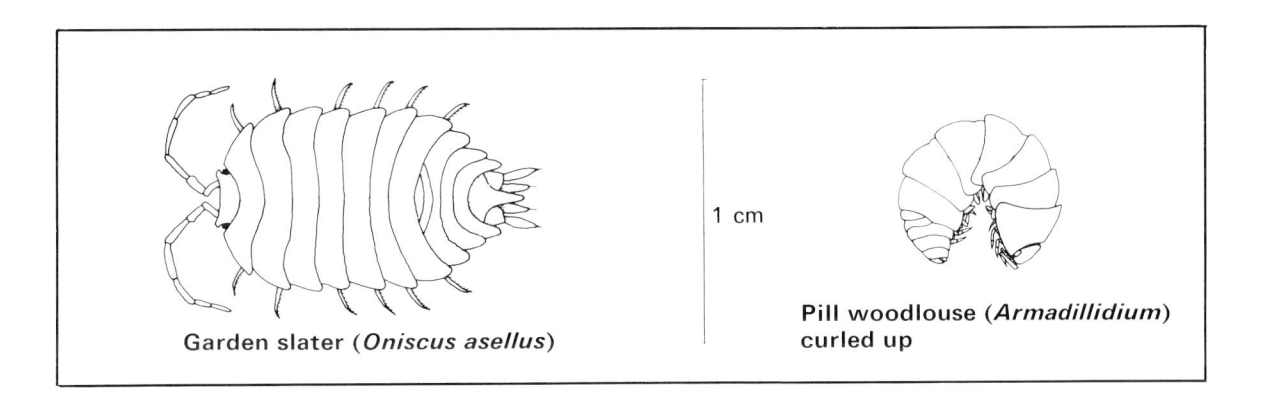

Garden slater (*Oniscus asellus*)

1 cm

Pill woodlouse (*Armadillidium*) curled up

Woodlice are easy to find and to keep. Although they belong to the group of animals called Crustaceans, the group that includes crabs, lobsters, shrimps and water-fleas, they live on land. There are several different kinds of woodlouse. One common kind is the pill woodlouse (*Armadillidium*) which is easily identified by its habit of rolling up into a ball when it is touched. No other kind of woodlouse does this. Another common kind is the garden slater (*Oniscus asellus*).

WHAT YOU NEED

Large flowerpot; sheet of glass to cover the pot; sheet of black cardboard; sheet of white blotting paper (or paper tissues). You will also need one or more containers for holding the woodlice while you are testing them. This can be a shallow glass or plastic dish 10 cm × 10 cm or bigger, with a sheet of glass to cover it. It is also possible to use a large ice-cream carton, cut as shown in the drawing.

GETTING STARTED

First prepare a home for the woodlice. Half fill the pot with moist soil, and put some damp rotting leaves or damp dead bark on top of the soil together with a slice or two of potato. If you want to watch the woodlice, rest the sheet of glass directly on the top of the pot. To keep the woodlice in complete darkness, put the black cardboard on the pot (black side down if it is black only on one side), then put the glass on top of this so that the weight of the glass presses the card firmly against the rim of the pot.

Look for woodlice in the garden, a park, a hedgerow or a wood. They are found in all kinds of damp, dark places. Look under large stones or logs, and in piles of bricks and rubble (provided it is damp). A damp log-pile is an excellent place for finding woodlice. Put the woodlice in a small plastic box, bottle or tube to carry them home, then set them free in the pot.

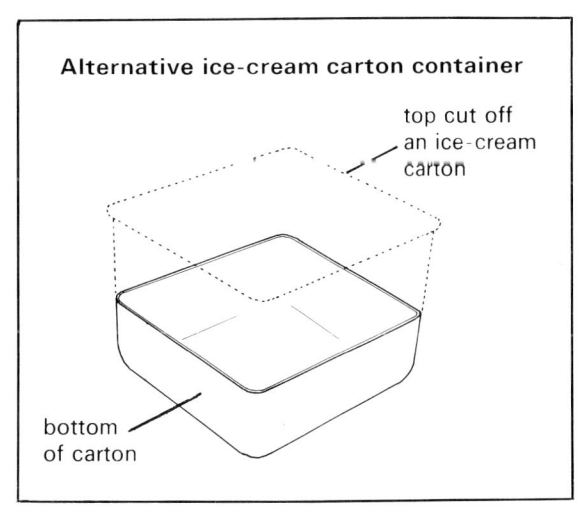

Alternative ice-cream carton container

top cut off an ice-cream carton

bottom of carton

Housing the woodlice

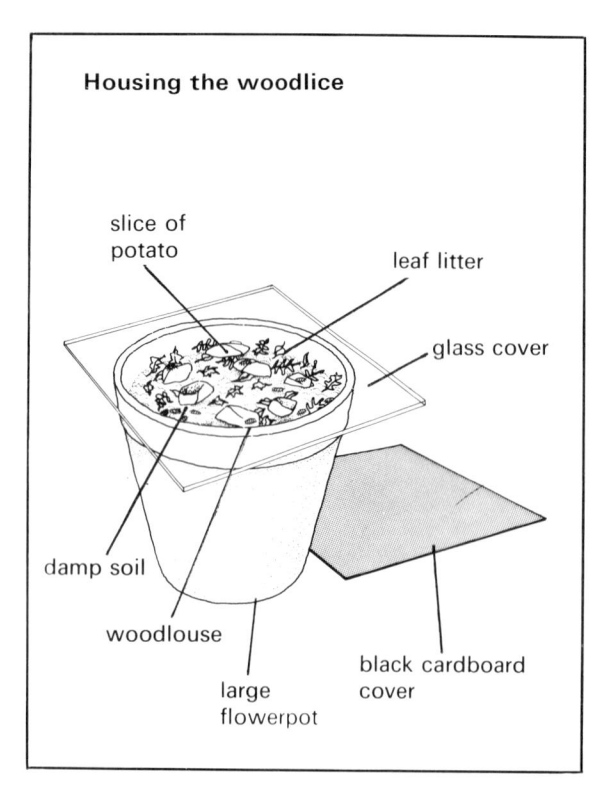

- slice of potato
- leaf litter
- glass cover
- damp soil
- woodlouse
- large flowerpot
- black cardboard cover

You may find more than one kind of woodlouse, but collect only one sort, about 20. If you want to make this into a big project, collect two or three different sorts (20 of each), but keep them in separate pots. Study each sort separately to see how they differ in their habits.

WHAT TO DO NEXT

Investigate the food preferences of woodlice. Put different kinds of food into the pot and leave it there overnight. On the next day, look to see how much has been eaten. It is best to use small amounts of food, for you might not notice tiny pieces nibbled here and there from a large lump. If you cut the food into neat cubes, you can more easily see where it has been eaten. Woodlice eat a wide variety of foods. Try them with potato, carrot, turnip, cabbage (cut cabbage or other leaves into neat squares), lettuce and meat of various kinds, including dead insects. You could also sow seeds, such as mustard and cress, in the pot and see if the woodlice eat the seedlings.

Woodlice feed mainly at night, so to see them actually feeding you need to look at them during the evening. Keep the black cover on the pot until you are ready to look at them. Do they feed at all times of night or just after dusk? By covering the pot during the day and by placing it *uncovered* beneath an electric lamp at night you could try to reverse their pattern of behaviour. You can turn day into night and night into day—this would make it much easier for you to study their feeding habits.

Woodlice breed well in captivity if their surroundings are kept damp and they have enough food. The females lay eggs in early summer and carry them around in a special brood pouch on the underside of the thorax. The young woodlice hatch in this pouch and stay there for a while. Then they leave the pouch and you will suddenly notice that a lot of small woodlice have been added to your colony. As they grow they moult several times. You can find the empty skins lying on the soil. Count the number of young woodlice. Work out how many woodlice you will have in 10 years' time if they continue to multiply at this rate.

Woodlice make good subjects for behaviour tests. You can try the same tests on other kinds of small animals too, including centipedes, millipedes, spiders (Chapter 1), earwigs, ants (Chapter 12), young snails, young slugs, maggots and earthworms (Chapter 6). You will find that different kinds of animal may behave in quite different ways.

Before beginning the experiments note the following points:

1. An animal that is unhealthy or dying or being badly treated will not respond properly so it is a waste of time trying to watch its behaviour. Use freshly caught animals or ones that you are keeping properly, using the methods described in this book. Also, do not do lots of tests on one animal. Give it a rest for several hours after each test.

2. Animals are individuals. They will not all behave alike. You should repeat each test at least ten times using a different animal of the same kind for each test. This is why you need at least 20 woodlice.

3. As soon as you have finished testing, put the animal back in its pot or cage. Animals that you have captured specially for testing should be set free immediately afterwards in the place from which they were taken.

BEHAVIOUR TESTS

Here are some questions that you can answer by trying tests with woodlice. The drawings help explain what to do.

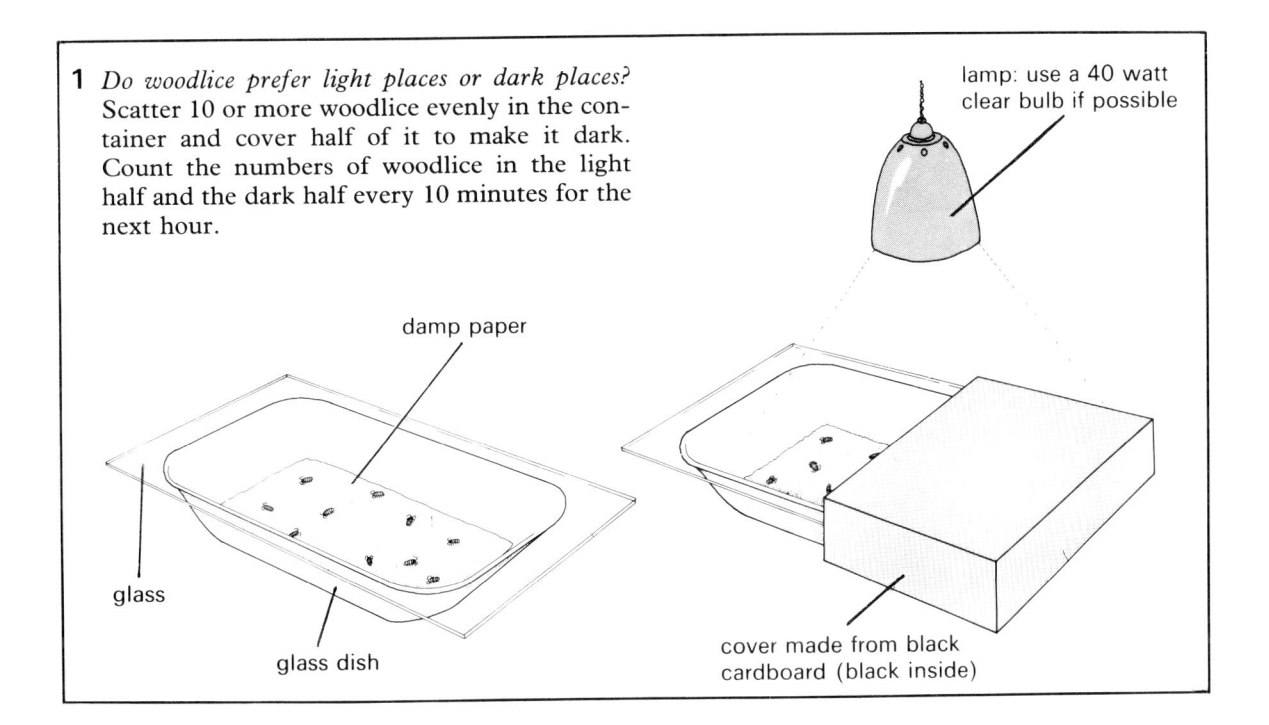

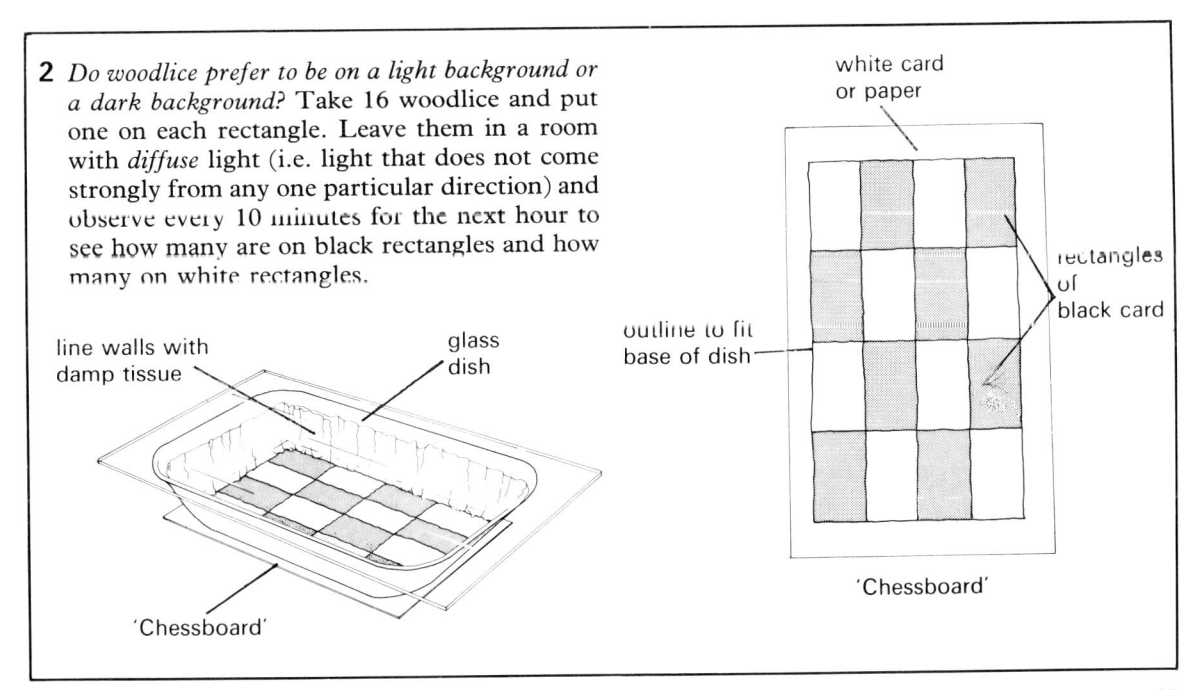

1 *Do woodlice prefer light places or dark places?* Scatter 10 or more woodlice evenly in the container and cover half of it to make it dark. Count the numbers of woodlice in the light half and the dark half every 10 minutes for the next hour.

2 *Do woodlice prefer to be on a light background or a dark background?* Take 16 woodlice and put one on each rectangle. Leave them in a room with *diffuse* light (i.e. light that does not come strongly from any one particular direction) and observe every 10 minutes for the next hour to see how many are on black rectangles and how many on white rectangles.

3 *Do woodlice prefer to crawl up or down a slope?* Place 10 woodlice half-way up the slope and cover the experiment to keep out light. See how many crawl up and how many crawl down. Repeat this three or four times with the same woodlice.

4 *How big a slope can a woodlouse detect?* Try the test above with the box sloped at different angles (5°, 10°, 15°, 20°, 25°, 30°). Find which is the least angle that affects the behaviour of the woodlice.

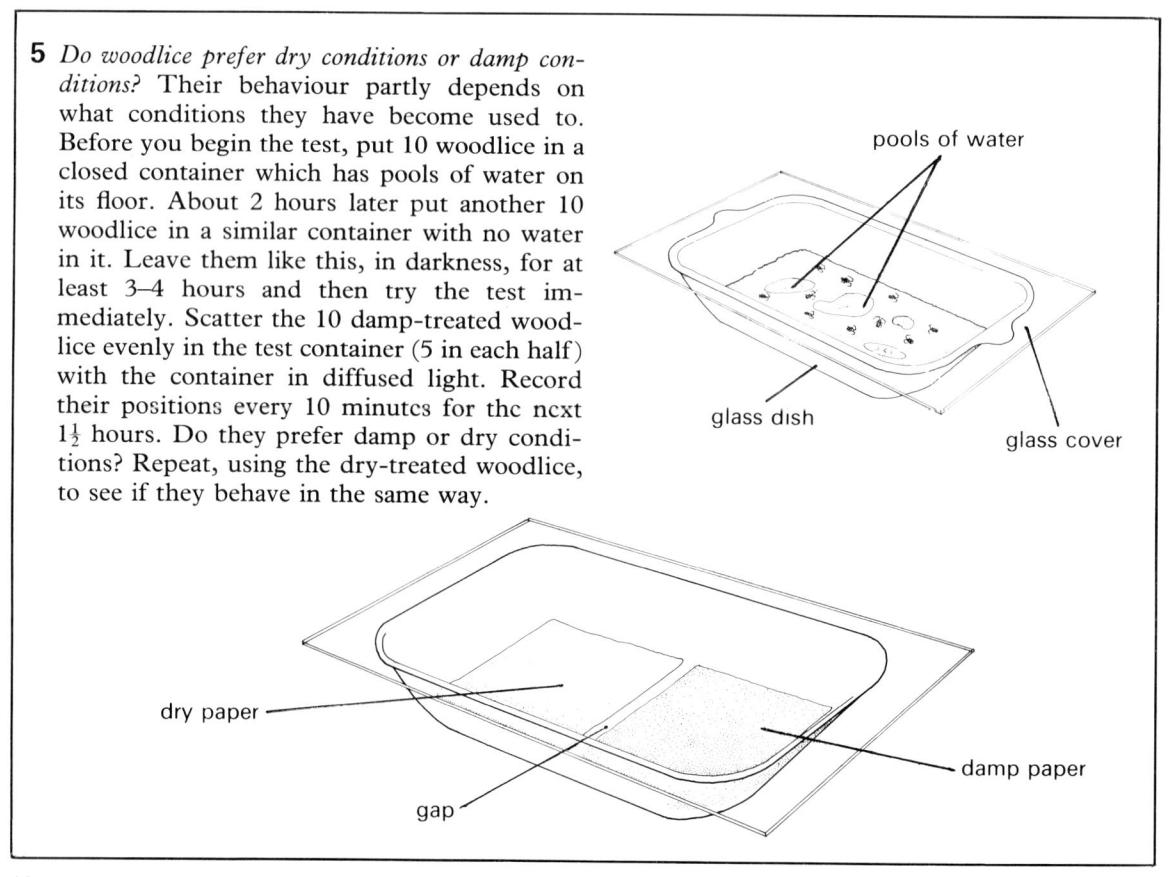

5 *Do woodlice prefer dry conditions or damp conditions?* Their behaviour partly depends on what conditions they have become used to. Before you begin the test, put 10 woodlice in a closed container which has pools of water on its floor. About 2 hours later put another 10 woodlice in a similar container with no water in it. Leave them like this, in darkness, for at least 3–4 hours and then try the test immediately. Scatter the 10 damp-treated woodlice evenly in the test container (5 in each half) with the container in diffused light. Record their positions every 10 minutes for the next 1½ hours. Do they prefer damp or dry conditions? Repeat, using the dry-treated woodlice, to see if they behave in the same way.

6 *How fast do woodlice crawl?* The grid is drawn in pencil on the blotting paper before it is dampened. On a similar but smaller grid, sketch the path of a woodlouse and measure the time it takes to travel this distance. To calculate the distance, lay a length of sewing thread along your sketch of its path and measure its length. Finally, work out its speed. Try this experiment with a damp-treated (see Question **5**) woodlouse first, in a box lined with damp tissue. Repeat with a damp-treated woodlouse in a box lined with dry tissue. Does dampness affect the speed of woodlice? Repeat this with several different woodlice to work out the average speed in the two conditions.

Repeat this section, using dry-treated woodlice to see if you get the same result. You could also do this with woodlice that have been kept in a refrigerator for 30 minutes.

7 *Do woodlice respond to the direction of light?* This experiment needs to be done in a darkened room. Try it with 10 woodlice one at a time, plotting all their tracks on the same sheet of paper. Does it make any difference if the woodlice are damp-treated or dry-treated? Does it make any difference if they are crawling on a damp surface or a dry surface?

8 *Do woodlice travel in straight lines?* You need a fairly large container in order to find the answer to this question. If your container is too small, try the test on an open board. Room lighting must be diffuse so that the direction of light can have no effect. Put a woodlouse on a damp surface, plotting its path for a fixed length of time (say 1 minute), and count the number of times it changes direction. Is the number of left turns roughly equal to the number of right turns? Repeat this for several woodlice. Now test some more woodlice, but on a dry surface. Does the number of turns per minute depend on whether the surface is damp or not?

If you had been walking in the rain in a straight line for 5 minutes and were still getting wet, you might reason that it would be a good idea to walk in some other direction in the hope of getting out of the rain. Although woodlice cannot reason as you can, does their behaviour seem to be based on the same idea?

(The lamp is only used in Test **7**)

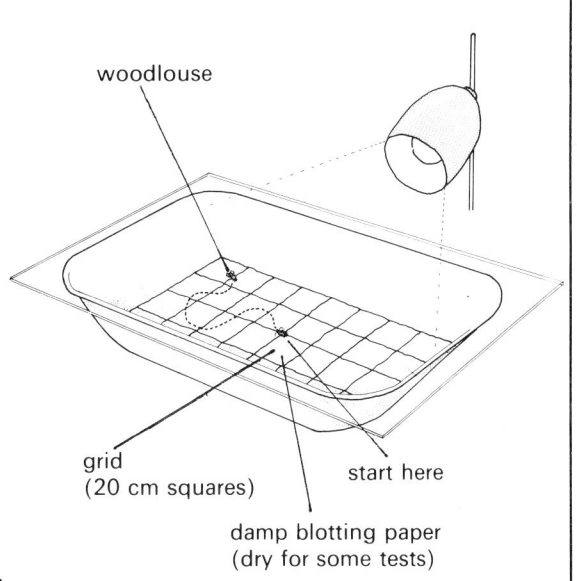

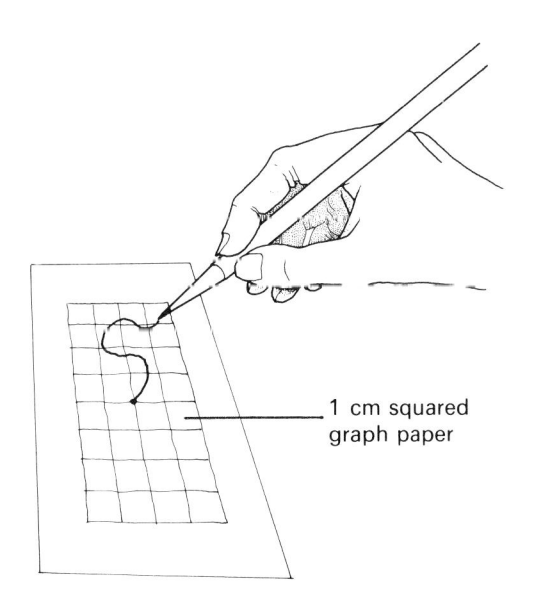

woodlouse

grid (20 cm squares)

start here

damp blotting paper (dry for some tests)

1 cm squared graph paper

11 Breeding flour beetles

Flour beetles live in and feed on stored flour. They are easy to keep and handle, which makes them suitable for breeding experiments.

WHAT YOU NEED

A stock culture of the *wild-type* flour beetle (*Tribolium castaneum*) and one of the *pearl eye type* flour beetle (see address p. 60); 1.5 kg bag of wholemeal flour; 80 g dried yeast (Four small 20 g sachets); two containers for the stock cultures (large jam jars or ice-cream cartons); several small containers for the breeding experiments—the best are 25 mm × 75 mm specimen tubes, but you can use test tubes, old aspirin bottles, or any glass or plastic container of similar size; fine muslin or similar fabric for covering the mouths of the containers; rubber bands (four large and several small ones); a kitchen sieve for separating insects from the flour (about twenty meshes to the inch); a small jar containing methylated spirits; a medium-sized water-colour paint-brush; a good hand-lens (× 8).

GETTING STARTED

First order your two stock cultures. While you are waiting to receive them prepare the flour and yeast mixture and the stock containers. Put the flour and yeast in a large *dry* mixing bowl and stir for at least 10 minutes to make sure the ingredients are well mixed. Transfer the mixture to an ovenware glass dish and heat in an oven for 30 minutes at 150 °C (300 °F) to sterilize it. Fill your two large stock containers about half-full of the mixture. Flour beetles do not need water but breed best in a damp atmosphere, so push a test tube or small jar containing water down into the flour. Be very careful not to spill any water into the flour or it will soon become mouldy. Cut pieces of muslin to fit over the rims of the containers and hold each of them in place with two large rubber bands. *Two* bands are used just in case one should break and let the beetles escape. Keep the remainder of the flour–yeast mixture for the breeding experiments. Flour beetles breed

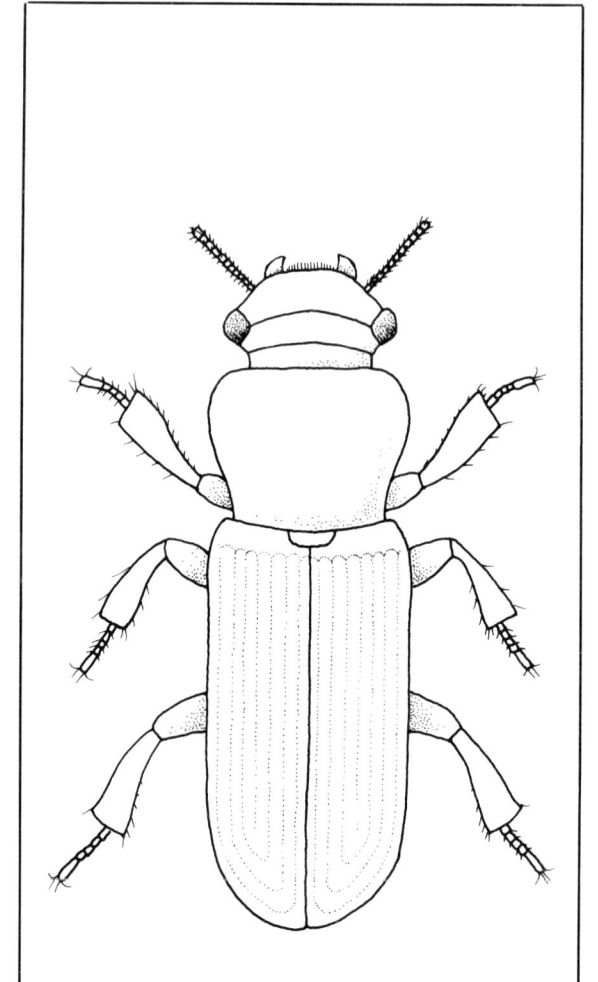

Adult flour beetle (*Tribolium castaneum*).
The beetle is about 4 mm long.

best at 25 °C, so you should try to find a warm room or cupboard where you can keep them for 3 or 4 months at least. An airing cupboard is very suitable for this.

Whenever you are handling the beetles take care that they do not escape, for they are pests and could find their way into the food cupboard. They do not fly at ordinary room temperatures and they crawl only slowly, so there will not be much danger of them crawling out of the container and escaping. Every time you work with the beetles spread a white cloth or a large sheet of white paper on the table. Then you will easily see any you have dropped which are trying to crawl away.

When the two stock containers are ready, label one 'Wild-Type' and the other 'Pearl Eye'. When the cultures arrive, study some beetles of each kind. Using the hand-lens, you can easily see the difference between the wild-type, with its *black* compound eyes, and the pearl eye beetles with their *white* eyes ringed with black. Tip one culture (the *whole* culture, *including the flour*) into each container, making sure you do not get them mixed. Cover the containers with the muslin making certain that there are no small crevices through which the beetles could escape. Put the containers in a warm place and leave them for a week. It does not matter if some or even all of the beetles have died before you receive the culture, as the culture contains plenty of live larvae and they will soon produce the pupae you need.

LOOKING AT THE STOCK CULTURES

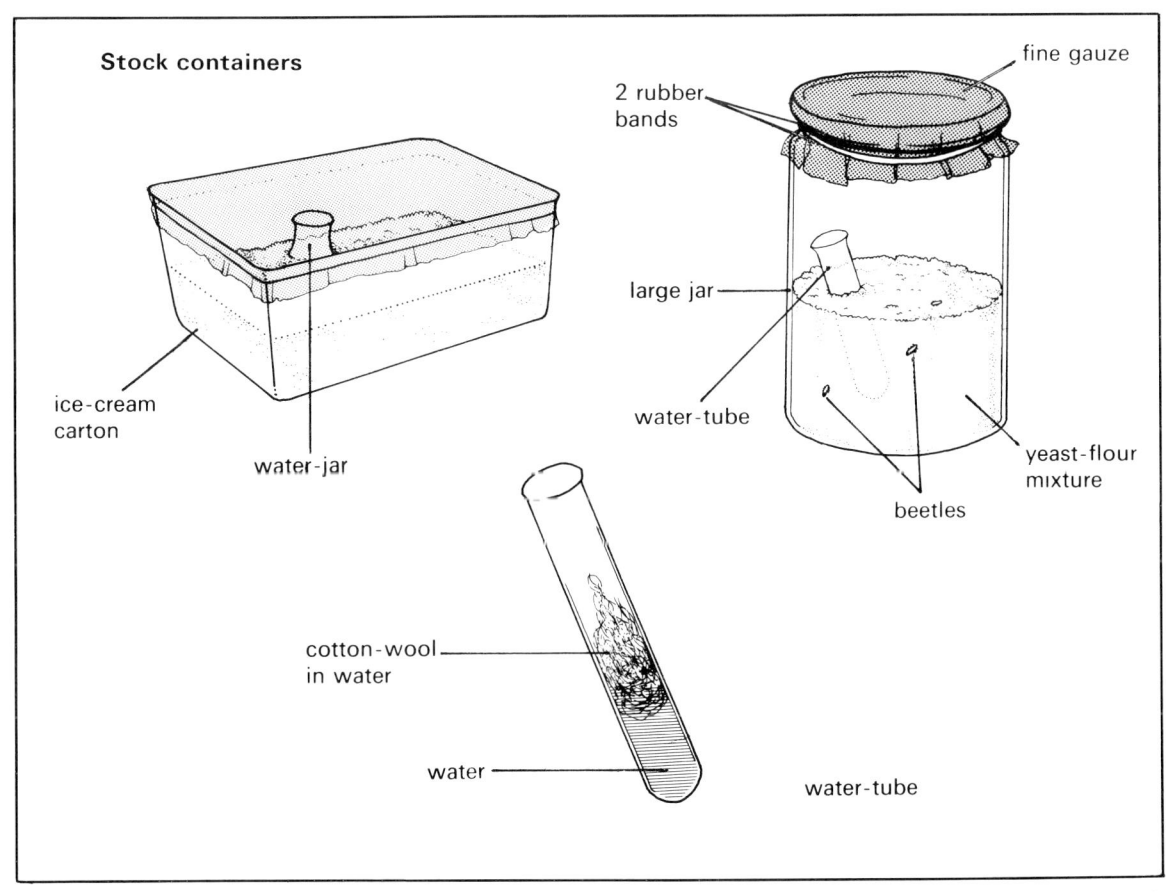

Each week sift through the flour, looking for the insects (remember to put the white cover on the table first). The first time you look you should find the original adults (if any) and maybe some pupae. There will be larvae too, but these are small and go through the sieve. One or two weeks later you should find a lot of pupae. Return all adults to the stock cultures, but keep most of the pupae for breeding. Always handle adults and pupae with a moist brush (see p. 35). Once you have found pupae there is no need to sift the stocks every week. If necessary, you can leave them for several months and the beetles will continue to feed and reproduce.

BREEDING

Put a little flour–yeast mixture in each of several tubes or small bottles. Tubes or bottles must be clean *and dry* before use. The aim is to have 6 male beetles and 6 female beetles in each tube. Some tubes should have wild-type males and pearl eye females while others should have wild-type females and pearl eye males. It is the *adults* that mate, but put *pupae* in the tubes. The reason for this is that if you put the female pupae in the tube *before* they hatch to the adult stage, you will ensure that females mate only with the type of male you put in the tube. (They will not have had the chance to mate with males from their own stock culture.) If you look carefully, you can tell the difference between a male pupa and a female pupa (see drawings). Into each breeding tube put 6 male pupae of one type (wild or pearl eye) with 6 female pupae of the other type.

Cover the tubes with muslin, held in place by two rubber bands, and put them in the same warm place as the stocks. To keep the air damp, put the tubes in a small closed box with a small jar of water in the box.

About 3 weeks later, sift the flour in each tube to find the adults that have hatched from the pupae, which you put in the tube. These are no longer needed and are best killed to prevent them from spreading to the food cupboard, so drop them into the methylated spirits jar.

The females will have laid eggs in the flour. The flour may now contain young larvae too. Put the flour back in the tube, clean the tube again and put it back in the warm place.

About 3 weeks later sift the flour in each tube again. By this time you should find plenty of pupae in the sieve. These are the offspring obtained by cross-breeding wild-type with pearl eye type. They are called the F_1 *generation*. Carefully put them back into the tubes and continue to sift the flour each week until you find that the adults have hatched. Use the hand-lens to look at these. How many of them have wild-type eyes (black) and how many have pearl eyes?

If your cross-breeding has been properly done, you should find *no* beetles with pearl eyes in this F_1 generation, as the pearl eye feature is *recessive* or 'hidden'. It does not show up in offspring from the cross between wild-type and pearl eye. Has the pearl eye feature simply disappeared? To

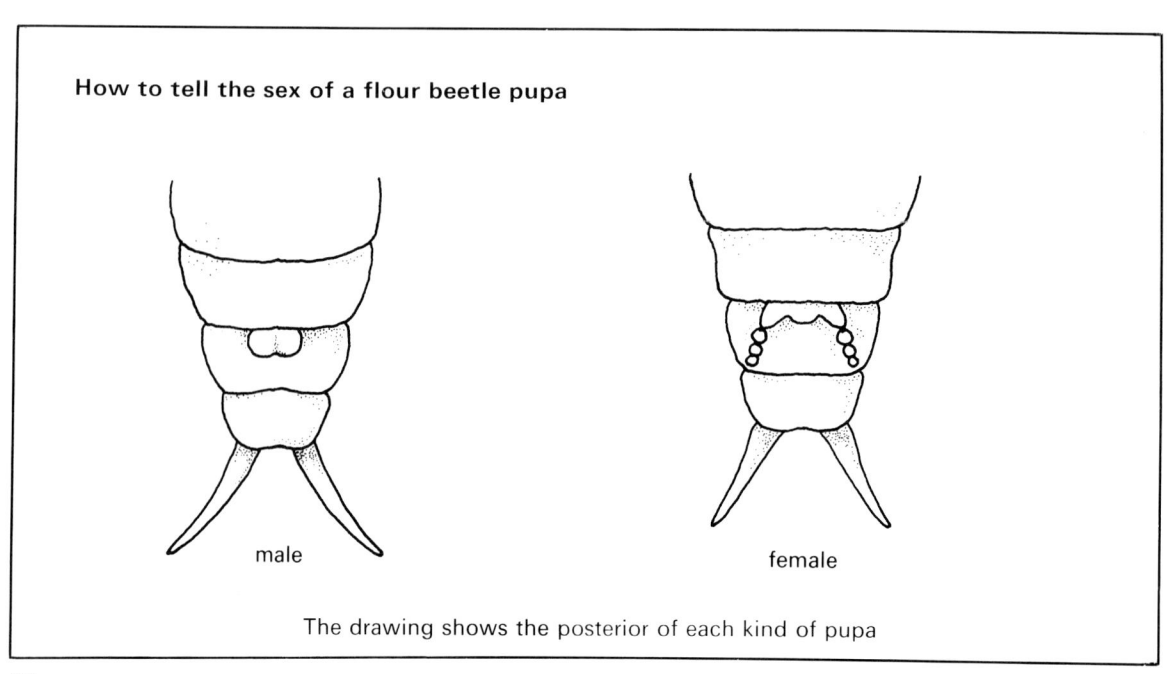

How to tell the sex of a flour beetle pupa

male

female

The drawing shows the posterior of each kind of pupa

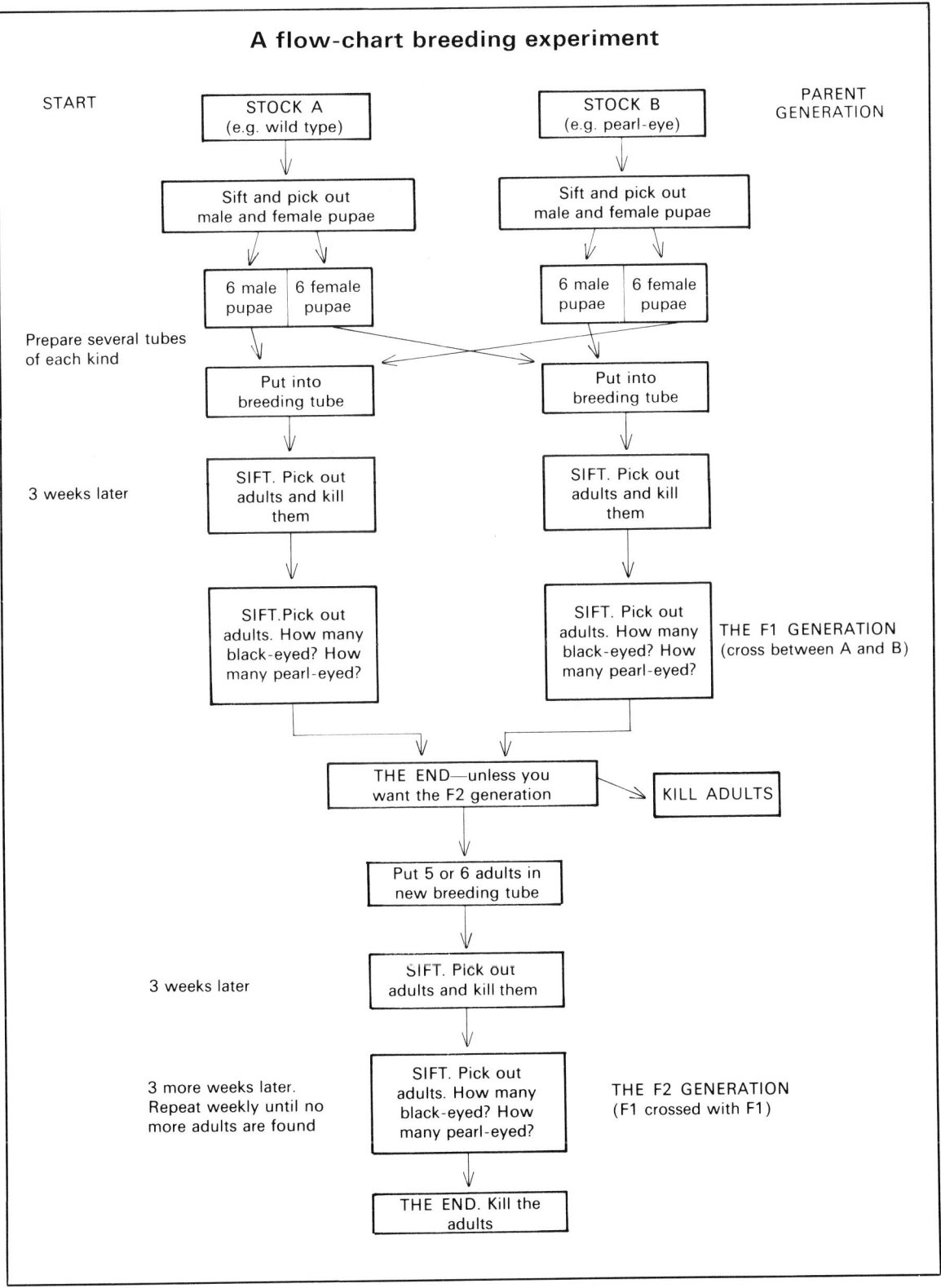

A flow-chart breeding experiment

```
START                STOCK A                      STOCK B              PARENT
                  (e.g. wild type)              (e.g. pearl-eye)       GENERATION
                        ↓                             ↓
                  Sift and pick out             Sift and pick out
                  male and female pupae         male and female pupae
                        ↓     ↓                       ↓     ↓
                  ┌──────┬──────┐              ┌──────┬──────┐
                  │6 male│6 female│            │6 male│6 female│
Prepare several   │pupae │pupae   │            │pupae │pupae   │
tubes of each     └──────┴──────┘              └──────┴──────┘
kind                    ↓   ⤨  ⤩                    ↓
                  Put into                     Put into
                  breeding tube                 breeding tube
                        ↓                             ↓
3 weeks later     SIFT. Pick out               SIFT. Pick out
                  adults and kill              adults and kill
                  them                         them
                        ↓                             ↓
                  SIFT. Pick out               SIFT. Pick out
                  adults. How many             adults. How many      THE F1 GENERATION
                  black-eyed? How              black-eyed? How       (cross between A and
                  many pearl-eyed?             many pearl-eyed?      B)
                        ↓                             ↓
                  THE END—unless you                    →  KILL ADULTS
                  want the F2 generation
                        ↓
                  Put 5 or 6 adults in
                  new breeding tube
                        ↓
3 weeks later     SIFT. Pick out
                  adults and kill them
                        ↓
3 more weeks later. SIFT. Pick out
Repeat weekly until adults. How many           THE F2 GENERATION
no more adults are  black-eyed? How            (F1 crossed with F1)
found               many pearl-eyed?
                        ↓
                  THE END. Kill the
                  adults
```

answer this it is necessary to breed the next generation, called the F_2 generation.

THE NEXT GENERATION

Transfer the F_1 adults that you have just bred to new tubes containing flour–yeast mixture. This time you will be breeding the F_1 adults with themselves, so you do not need to pick out pupae first. Put 5 or 6 adults in each tube. Three weeks later they will have mated and eggs will have been laid. At this stage sift the flour, take out the adults and kill them. After about 3 weeks, more of the larvae will have turned into pupae and some of them will have hatched into adults. Look at the tubes weekly to collect the adults of the F_2 generation. Each time, count how many wild-type adults you find and how many pearl eye adults. Kill the adults after you have counted them. You will now see that the pearl eye feature has not been lost. Find the total number of adults of each type. What fraction of adults of the F_2 generation has pearl eye? The answer and explanation is on p. 58.

OTHER EXPERIMENTS

Here are some more cross-breeding experiments to do. Try and predict the results, and then try the cross.

1 Cross some of your F_1 generation with the wild-type stock. You must use F_1 *pupae* (not adults) with stock *pupae*.

2 Cross some of your F_1 generation with the stock pearl eye type. Use F_1 *pupae* with stock *pupae*.

The supplier from whom you bought the stock probably sells stocks of other types. These may include 'black' which has a black body, 'sooty' with a dull black body, 'antennapedia' with forked antennae and 'microcephalic' which has a small head, as if a piece has been bitten out of each side. Do not get more than one new culture at a time, for there are plenty of experiments to be done with each culture.

You can also study the rate of increase of the beetles, as described for aphids in Chapter 4.

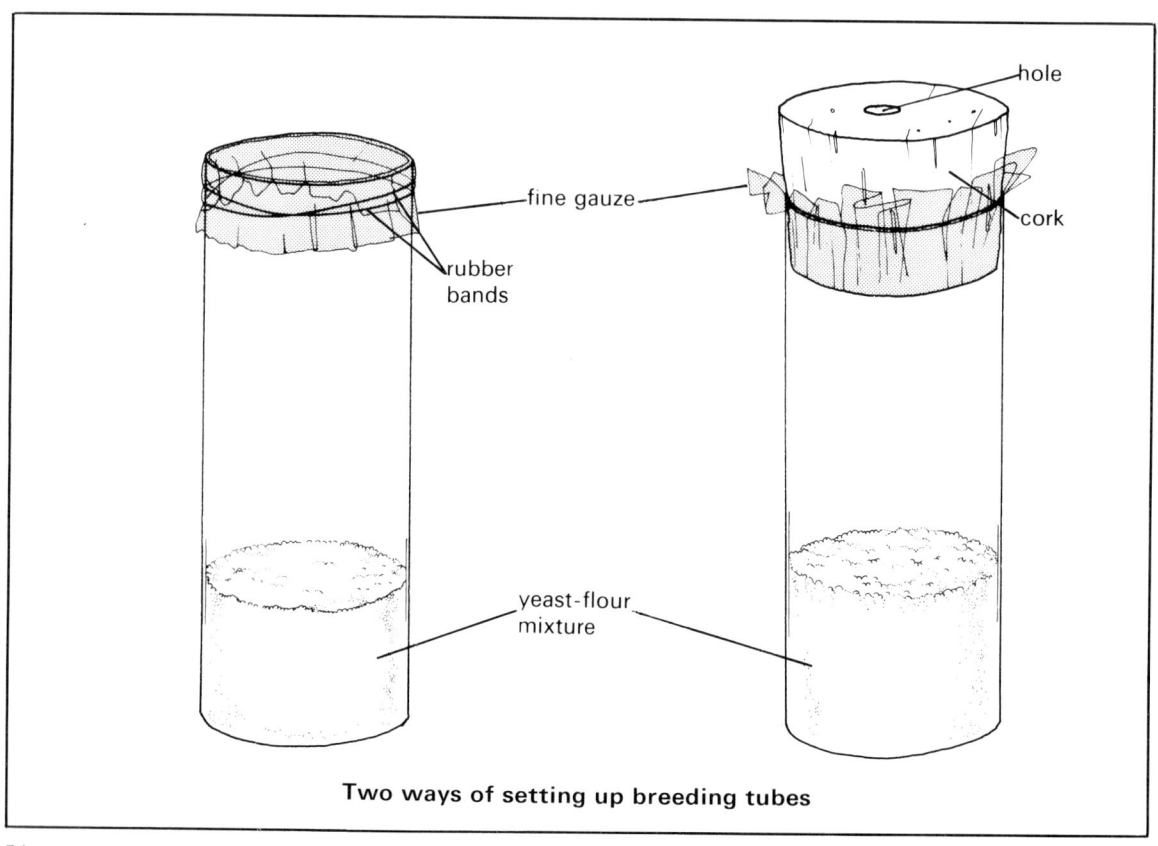

Two ways of setting up breeding tubes

12 Keeping ants

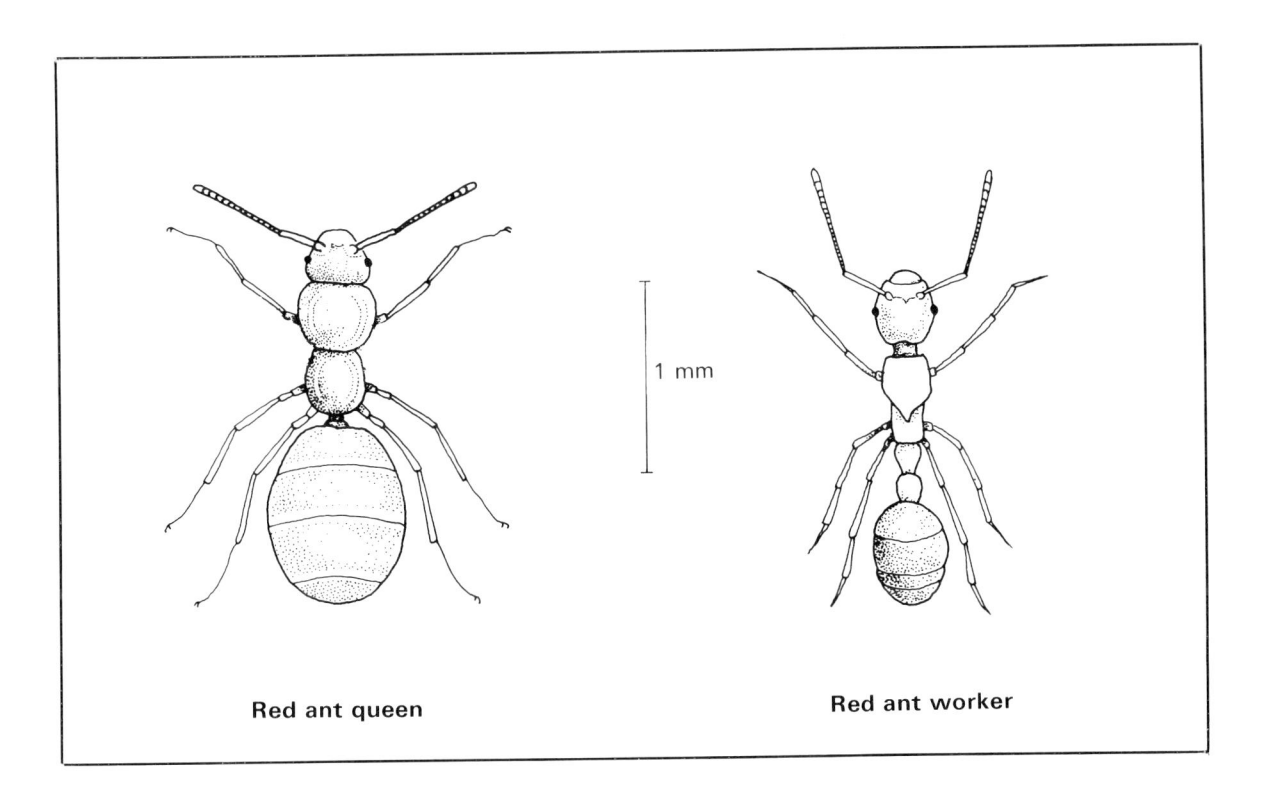

Red ant queen

1 mm

Red ant worker

Ants can be kept in large glass jars filled with soil or in a wormery (Chapter 6), but to see them best you should keep them in a special kind of housing. This is known as a *formicarium*.

WHAT YOU NEED

A kilogram or two of surgical plaster or plaster-of-Paris depending on the size of the housing (you can buy powdered plaster at a chemist's shop); a dish to act as a mould for casting the plaster block—the dish can be any size from 10 cm × 20 cm up to about 20 cm × 20 cm, but should have a flat bottom and sides that slope slightly outward; a sheet of glass to cover the housing; a sheet of black cardboard; Plasticine; small blocks of wood or small plastic boxes (the round boxes used for typewriter ribbons are very suitable); cotton-wool.

GETTING STARTED

First prepare the mould. The housing is to be cast upside down. Put *a drop* of cooking oil in the dish and use your finger to smear it over the bottom and the lower areas of the sides. Lay out the small, smooth wooden blocks or small boxes where the living compartments for the ants are to be. You can also use large flat discs of Plasticine to mould the compartments. You can choose the layout to suit yourself, but keep these points in mind:

1 There should be at least three compartments for the ants to live in.

2 There should be one reasonably large feeding compartment. This *must* be at one end of the housing, clear of the other compartments, and then you will be able to slide the glass off this compartment without sliding it off the others.

3 The compartments should be joined to each other by corridors. Add these to the mould by rolling out 'worms' of Plasticine, 5–10 mm in diameter, and join the blocks together with these worms. One worm should lead from the feeding compartment to one of the other compartments.

4 Put one or two well compartments at the side of the block (more if the housing is large). These are *not* to be connected to the other compartments.

Oil the blocks or boxes before putting them in position.

When all is ready, mix the plaster as follows. Put the dry plaster in a bowl and add some water, a *little at a time*, stirring all the time until the plaster is *just* sloppy enough to pour. Put the dish on a level table and then pour the plaster gently into the dish. The level should be about 5 mm above the highest of the blocks. Leave the dish undisturbed overnight.

Since the dish has sloping sides, the block of plaster should slide out easily. Remove the boxes and Plasticine, and tidy up the rough edges, using a craft knife. The housing is now ready to receive the ants.

FINDING ANTS

One of the best types of ant to keep is the red ant. This is common on waste land, grassy areas and in meadows. Since each colony of red ants has several queens, you will not have too much difficulty in getting a queen for your colony. You can often find a colony by looking under large flat stones, planks of wood or rubble lying on the soil. When you find a colony you will see thousands of ants, some carrying eggs or grubs. Use a trowel to scoop up some of these and put them in a plastic bag. Look among the ants for one that is larger than the others—this will be the queen. If you have not found a queen, your colony will not survive for long, so try again. Try not to put any soil in the bag with the ants.

The most difficult operation is transferring the ants to the housing, and is best done out of doors. Have the housing ready with the glass covering all the compartments except the feeding compartment (see drawing). You can try tipping the ants (but no soil) into the feeding compartment. Some ants may be lost but make sure that the queen goes in. Then slide the glass *slowly* across to cover the compartment. If the compartment is large enough and the bag is small enough, you can put the whole bag in the compartment, tear a

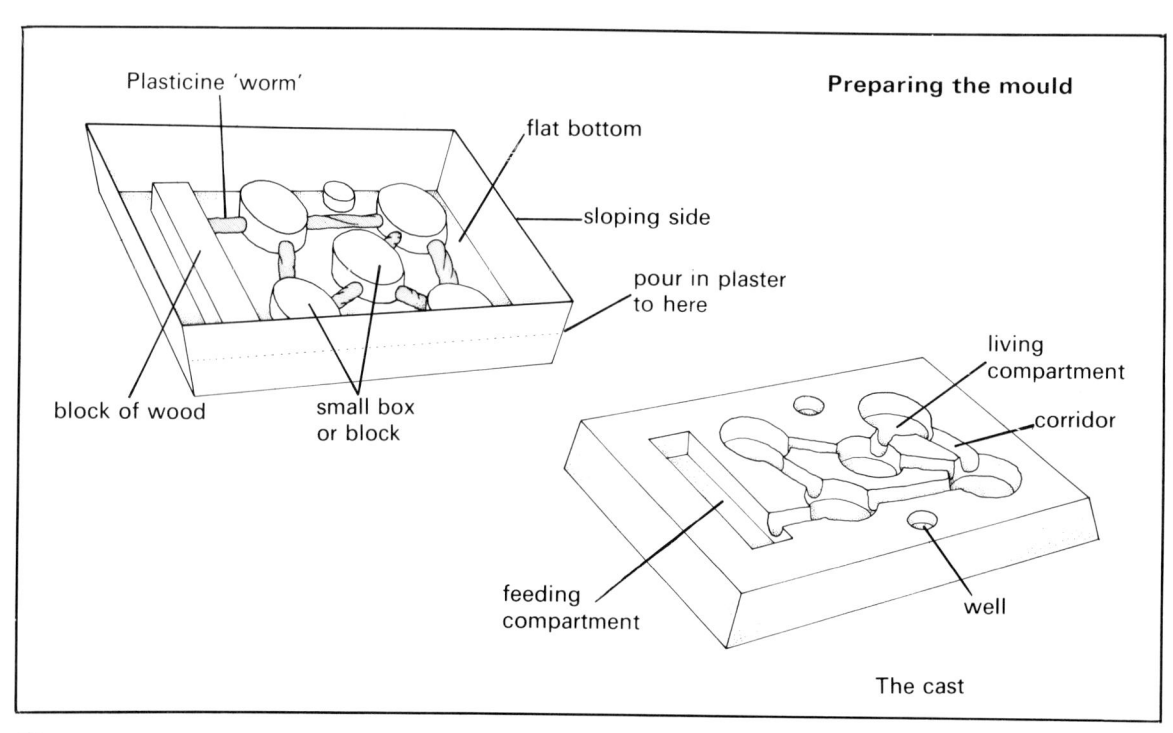

Preparing the mould

Plasticine 'worm', flat bottom, sloping side, pour in plaster to here, block of wood, small box or block

living compartment, corridor, feeding compartment, well

The cast

small hole in it and immediately slide the glass across before the ants have had time to escape. Later, when the ants are gone, you can remove the bag.

LOOKING AFTER THE ANTS

The ants will soon find their way into the living compartments and begin to set up their colony there. It is best to cover the glass with the sheet of black cardboard when you are not actually observing the ants—the feeding compartment is always left uncovered. The housing should be kept moist by pouring a little water into the wells from time to time. Since the wells are at the edge of the block, you will be able to slide the glass to one side to fill the wells. It is important always to *slide* the glass, *never* lift it off the block. If you do, the ants will climb out on to the upper surface of the block and you will not be able to replace the glass without crushing many of the ants.

To feed the ants, wait until the feeding compartment is empty. Then *slide* the glass back to open the chamber and quickly close the entrance hole with a plug of cotton-wool. Place some cotton-wool soaked in sugar solution on the floor of the feeding compartment, remove the plug and slide the glass back into position. Other foods that can be placed in the compartment include caterpillars and small insects. You could also try introducing greenfly on some rose twigs (Chapter 4). It is interesting to discover which are the ants' favourite foods.

Clean out the feeding compartment from time to time. The ants will bring dead ants and other unwanted rubbish from their nests and throw them into the feeding compartment. Remove this rubbish, old pieces of sugared cotton-wool and other remains of uneaten food.

Ants are social insects, so their life is a fairly complicated one. There is plenty for you to watch: the way they feed, the way they cluster around the queen, the way they look after their eggs and grubs (larvae), the development of the larvae into adult ants. Ask in your Public Library or School Library for books about ants. These will give you ideas on what to look for while you are watching your colony.

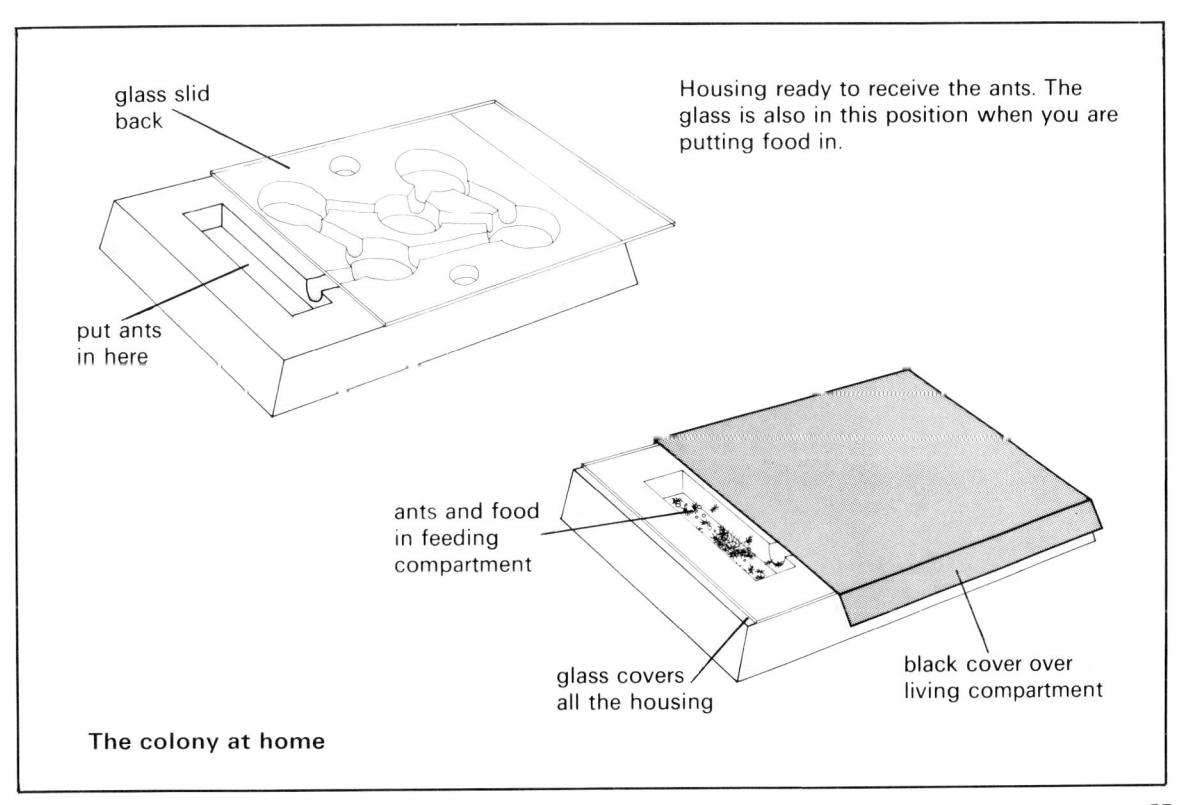

glass slid back

put ants in here

Housing ready to receive the ants. The glass is also in this position when you are putting food in.

ants and food in feeding compartment

glass covers all the housing

black cover over living compartment

The colony at home

RESULTS OF BREEDING FLOUR BEETLES

Each beetle carries two factors (or genes) that determine the colour of its eyes. Beetles can have pearl eyes only if *both* of the two genes are for pearl eyes. If both genes are for wild-type eyes, or one is for wild-type and one for pearl eye, the beetle has wild-type (black) eyes. A beetle can pass only *one* gene to each of its offspring. So if a beetle carries both types of gene, about half of its offspring receive a wild-type gene and half receive a pearl eye gene.

When you cross pure breeding (++) wild-type beetles with pure breeding (pp) pearl type beetles, all the F_1 generation are (+p); they *carry* the pearl gene but *look* wild-type.

When you cross these F_1 beetles with each other, there are *four* possible ways of pairing genes from the two parents (see drawing). Three of these four ways give black-eyed beetles of the F_2 generation and only one way gives pearl eye. These four ways are equally likely to happen so the expected ratio of black-eyed and pearl-eyed beetles is *3 to 1*.

For further explanation see *Genetics for 'O' Level* by J. J. Head and N. R. Dennis (Oliver and Boyd).

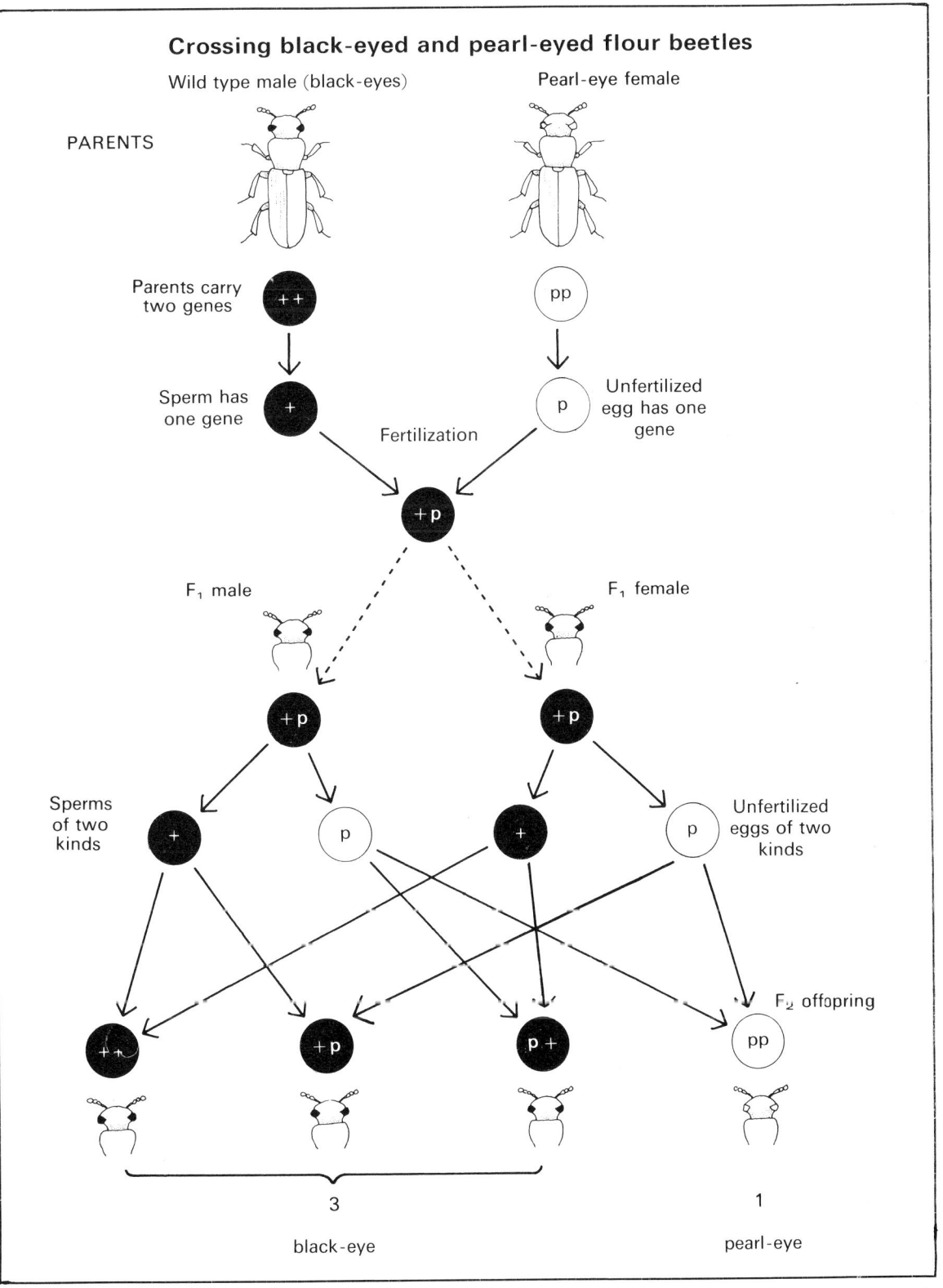

Crossing black-eyed and pearl-eyed flour beetles

SOME USEFUL BOOKS

The Pocket Encyclopaedia of Plant Galls by Arnold Darlington (Blandford Press).
The World of a Tree by Arnold Darlington (Faber and Faber).
The Observer's Book of Butterflies by W. J. Stokoe (Warne).
Studying Insects by R. L. E. Ford (Warne).
Genetics for 'O' Level by J. J. Head and N. R. Dennis (Oliver and Boyd).
Name this Insect by E. F. Daglish (Dent).
Insects in Colour by N. D. Riley (Blandford).
Butterflies, Moths and their Caterpillars by George E. Hyde (Warne's Picture Reference Books).
Water Animal Identification Keys by J. Eric Marson (School Natural Science Society, available from Publications Officer, Association for Science Education, College Lane, Hatfield, Herts, AL10 9AA).

EQUIPMENT SUPPLIERS

The Butterfly Farm Ltd, Bilsington, Ashford, Kent, TN25 7JW.
World Wide Butterflies Ltd, Over Compton, Sherborne, Dorset, DT9 4QN.
Griffin and George Ltd, Gerrard Biological Centre, Worthing Road, East Preston, West Sussex, BN16 1AS. Telephone: Rustington (09062) 72071. (For eggs and larvae of white butterflies, cultures of flour beetle, plankton, nets, larvae cages and other items of equipment.)
Philip Harris Biological Ltd, Oldmixon, Weston-super-Mare, Avon, BS24 9BC. (For butterfly eggs and larvae, cultures of flour beetle and other items of equipment.)